T0129687

Destiny 2

.

Destiny 2

Hairi Lasisi

iUniverse, Inc.
Bloomington

Destiny 2
Destiny

Copyright © 2012 by Hairi Lasisi.

All rights reserved. No part of this book may be used or reproduced by any means, graphic, electronic, or mechanical, including photocopying, recording, taping or by any information storage retrieval system without the written permission of the publisher except in the case of brief quotations embodied in critical articles and reviews.

iUniverse books may be ordered through booksellers or by contacting:

iUniverse
1663 Liberty Drive
Bloomington, IN 47403
www.iuniverse.com
1-800-Authors (1-800-288-4677)

Because of the dynamic nature of the Internet, any web addresses or links contained in this book may have changed since publication and may no longer be valid. The views expressed in this work are solely those of the author and do not necessarily reflect the views of the publisher, and the publisher hereby disclaims any responsibility for them.

Any people depicted in stock imagery provided by Thinkstock are models, and such images are being used for illustrative purposes only.
Certain stock imagery © Thinkstock.

ISBN: 978-1-4759-4055-8 (sc)
ISBN: 978-1-4759-4056-5 (ebk)

Library of Congress Control Number: 2012913113

Printed in the United States of America

iUniverse rev. date: 07/26/2012

Contents

God Is Great

God is able to do anything, believe in God, what ever religion you are in, believe that God is able to do above exceeding what we can think of. God create heaven and earth, but the heaven is a paradise.

We saw the Earth and the Sun. The Moon is the reflection from the sun. That is the two planet we can see through our eyes without the telescope on earth. That is the planet reveal to humans, and the Moon make the third. The question is who can go to the sun, nobody, not even our human created gadget can enter the sun, they will burnt away. Could the sun be compare to heaven!, disguise like a moon!, a paradise that know human can go to.

The God also show us that this Earth carry its milk and water and everything humans possibly need to growth. The sun reflect to humans on earth and we reflected back to sun. God create man and woman to bring something out beautiful.

The God also show us by creating black and white from his color. We were born, leaves and die.

The innocent night hawk, Shoppers, my sincere appreciation to everyone who helped to provide information and photographs for this book.

The Season

The season always come and go. Summer will come, the whole area will be hot creating a lot of heat for some months. The fall will also come, and all the leafs will come down from the tree for some months. It all temporary, nothing still, it evolve the circle of live. Through to the winter that will be very cold. The body temperature change and that takes us back to the summer again. The tree leafs begin again. We could not say that these season happen all over the world. This type of weather changes occur in America and Europe. The Africa weather pattern is totally difference from what I am talking about in this book. The leafs never come down from the tree because of the weather.

INTRODUCTION

This book is a continuation of a Destiny, the old version of this book. It explain in more details the psyche encounter and the intelligence of the society. The norms explain the way of the society and their culture. How people behave and the belief that bind them together. Years of research and examination of case studies reveals that after damaging to any part of our body, soul can result in abnormal situation. Now, I am not saying it can not be fixed by doctors or any healer for that matter, but we must be careful to use our body.

As it has been argued many times, humans state of mind can be altered by natural changes in our souls and in the earth's magnetic fields. The same changes that can produce spectacularly varied in physical and visual geographical effects. The alien experience in another world can be a demo-stating to that effects.

BIRTH PLACE

CHAPTER ONE

Every one can remember his birth place, they might not remember their date of birth but they will remember where they were born. The place where I was born was a quiet place with about the population of 2,000 to 5,000 people. I live in this town for some years. I was educated in this town also for some years. I completed my primary education in this town before moving out. I can not recollect my early childhood but I can recollect my childhood when I started going to school at the age of six. I love this town because it is nice but the people are not good for themselves, they mean too much to themselves, they quarrel all the time, perhaps fighting is good sometimes to express themselves. They have chief and chief township title in this town that control the affairs of the town only when the situation beyond their control of their chiefs then they call police to enforce the law and go to court, otherwise the chief settle most of the case for the people of this town.

I have many friends in this town, mostly I can not remember them till today, may be I can remember a few of them, because we all get old, and the face changes. I go out a lot with my friends, no fight between us, sometime we ague about some thing and that is all. This little town is the heart of the other town in the area, occasionally, I go from one town to another, most people of this town getting rich an that mean they were influence in a good jobs and politics around them. They started to develop this town with their own money by building a new roads, new houses, power house and much more. The people were ambitious to move forward. After school I have another lesson to go to in the evening to sturdy another language which is totally different from the English language that we use and learn in the school. Sometimes I came out from school late and if I have any assignment to do in the school, after I finish from the lesson class in the evening, I will have to go to a water place to go and fetch water for my parents, and that will be use in the house, from the shallow water, the spring water, the water people of the town use for their drinking water, the water place is like a pound it does run, the water is full of snakes and small fish that support the water. On the evening of any festival the water will go down from the pond because many people come to fetch water on till the people are less to fetch water, I wonder how this water could support the town, but to reveal the secret is to tell the people that understand why the water have to operate that way, or to ask the intelligent people. Also I will have to come home and prepared to cook for the people in the house, and after I finish cooking and eat dinner with my family, then I will sturdy for some hours before I go to bed at night.

During the time, there is civil war going on in our country. The federal solder is on our side and the government is been telling everybody not to go out and play anyway or just been playing around as they use to because of unaware of the hidden bomb. I like going out with my father, and my friends. My father was a chief in our town, a chief have to face his own duty as every other chiefs, so as been a chief, he is too old for the army. What causes the war at that time was unknown to me but the elders of the town know better. I was too young, I can not be recruited in the army either. I wasn't getting the full information about what is going on. The army was never give the full account of what happen during the war anyway, but they do aware how the money is been spend. The rebel attack the city first, the rebel army send signal that they are ready to engage in a war with federal government, now the federal government realized that they are at war with rebel. The federal army was never intension to fight the rebel because they are the same country, and for the rebel, they want to break away from the federal government without the proper procedure that acceptable to each other.

To break away from the federal government without proper procedure that will be acceptable to each other means the rebel have a chance to control the whole government main resources and the federal will be left for nothing. The federal government is more populated and bigger in size than the rebel, but because they are fortunate to have the main resources on their side give them boost and flamboyant to engage war with the federal which at last result in lost by the rebels. Now that the federal government realize that they can not lose resources to the rebels, they gain the upper hands, the federal will have to fight the rebels. The war goes for many years, many people was enlist on the army list, I can not be listed because of my age was below the minimum age, and the army school was not easy to get into unless you know the officers or someone at the recruitment department, and in this case, I know no one at the army recruitment department, so I did not worry much about it. At last the federal government won the war and control the whole country side including all of the resources. During the war, many things change, there is a scares of foods, short of labors even goat hunting, everyone know that the life of goat head will not be that demanded and lives the with a great time of trouble to read. In your dream can you buy something from the one that you support and lives the one that you messing with, that is not meant for you! This is a clear case of a political injustice of a dream, must dream.

When you are a kid, you probably recognize every thing that happen or that you did, but sometimes you are the innocent of it. A kid of one year or two that can crawl to anywhere is an innocent of what he or she did. When you also do something weather you are adult a man and you are not purposely or intend to do it means you are also an innocent. A child playing with toilet or dust of any poising and other household danger is an innocent of it because those danger is not recognizable to him, if she know how danger it was, she will know better as a kid. An innocent until proven guilty, that means when you know that what you did is wrong or not wrong but will have to accept that you are wrong when continue doing the same thing over and over again. The man or the chiefs has little experience of what they are doing, even sometimes experience from their predecessor and ancestor to judge the case for the people of the town and you are there at that time thinking they are very good, but when you finally reach that stage, then you realize that it is not so that bad or rather or rather is difficult to judge some one with clear or no clear evidence.

Innocent between the black man and white man case. The old idea that watch each other steps for the purpose of position, employment and politics. The innocent man can see all this as a game play and turn himself into a game scene of power ranger. Human idea is easy to sticky it with, other humans. Once they practice it and research it and it set to works, is like a migraine medicine that was practice and research and discover and became valuable and everyone can use it. Some people stop at nothing that means they do not care if they are dealing with animals or humans, and some people simply does not know any better when to stop for a bad things until the war broke out. The war is inevitable, it will happen if it has to, but good thinking can prevent must of the mistakes and the love of other people.

The idea of two man or two and half men was made by a comedian known as for the two men living together and raising a boy kids, that means the boy will have to listen to both of the men in the house, maybe that may guarantee for the success of the boy. When two racist mixed together they produce the third one, these type of situation can be carry out when things are sufficient for both of them, but beside that, all kind of unhealthy situation can be carry out and also resulted in a fight and name calling. Children can be misplay when you don't know what you are doing, you think is a play or what the elders was saying is not good for society. Despite that some culture can not turn back in time to become a normal people such as gay couple, bisexual marriages which is a total outrageous in our society today. Some state even pass the law to be public act such as gays and bisexuals. The children can carry that derrick or a bur ding of some culture, to be a child play of some type of behavior means your father is not in that categories of that culture and while your mother was also not in that culture but for some reason, it became a child abuse of a some culture because you don't like what they practice but because you were blind about it, it became something to think about.

Sexual connotation, many children do not aware what sex is all about, sex is very good when you married to it or know what you are doing for fun or not for fun. Misbehave about sexuality can also cause you pain and grieve because when you are doing sex you totally forget about the unfair part of it until you are finished doing it, sucks you regret it for the rest of your life. If you know more than that, that you were born into a culture, then it is to analyze if you were to follow that culture or adopt a new one or better one such as religion. If you are christian it can be easy to change to another religion if you fell you need something to gain from it, but in many culture child abuse is very common among the society.

Consider this scenario in the life of human being. The time dream that says at every certain of time in the night that you must dream, that is from devil, devil will never let you rest, he knows when you are sleeping and when you are not. When you are in the building doing your job but at night you must forgets sleep, you never knew what making you to fall asleep what you deter min to be on the job, the snow fox that was near you at night or raccoon that looking for food all around you. The brain is small to be worry about all that, never think if you are station on info red light all day long. For a serious person that want to work or working must put every thing in consideration and know what to do in the case of anything happen.

When I was in Nigeria, I got a job at willisco company. We are many called for the interview as industrial radiographer. I was not even hope for anything, not until they started conducting an interview, we are about twenty people contestant for the job. I know that willisco want to hire as many as he can to keep the job going. Out of twenty contestant the first round, round up at ten people, the second round, round up at five people, and I am among of those five people. They finish the interview and we start working. As a training we will have to go through training for six months before we become the staff member. Not many people can take that chances of going through training before they can start making money, they have bills to pay, and have other responsibilities to take care off. Another guy quite due to the money. Immediately I started working they bring another man from London which happen to be white, Mr Thompson. The company already have a white dude that was working with them. The job was going fine. Mr. Thompson was a gentleman but he like women and like to enjoy himself, sometimes he will get drunk and will not be able to performed on the job, he knows the job alright but is not willing to learn the habit of environment. When he arrived we all welcome him and try sheer him up. As the company started loosing from customer and Mr. Thompson started making too much noises, the company gave him a warning letter that they will return him back to London if he did not face his job, but he refuse to listen, so as soon as contract expired the company send him back to London.

Furthermore, for we apprentice, the first employee quite, said he get another job on advertising business, now remain four apprentice me and other three employee. When two of them left the company to another company, then fortunately I get a job at another company also, and the company will pay more money, more benefits. The job at willisco is good only if I can finish the training, but not many people can go through that endurance. The remain employee, I don't know how they make out.

Immediately I join the new company, I like my boss and my boss like me. I quickly associate myself with those guy I met there, the white manager I met there do not like me much, but he never catch me doing something bad. Sometimes I will feel like sleeping on the job and this white guy will be coming with the hope that he will caught me while I am sleeping; but before he gets to me; I was already awake and he would look at me like saying something. He would just walk pass me; and ask me I'm sleeping! I will say no, off-cause not, sleeping on the job!, not me, I know I was sleeping on the job, sleeping on the job is a problem to me, even as I was getting older; is still given me problem, no matter how many cup of coffee I may drink, I will still be sleeping. Sometimes I will take my shoes off and my sucks, so that I walk around with my bear foot but sometimes that does stopping me from sleeping. I do not like noises making, I prefer to be in a quiet area so I can do my job properly, but at the same time I do get a job in an industries where it full of machines working at the same time and that is a lot of noises.

Moving to another place is good, however considering the encounter with alcohol people, people you never knew and they can blow anything on your face, the attitude of the outsider and the freedom fighter in all dangerous places. At work is to meet new people that you going to be dealing with everyday and also old baby boomer, they have many children to protect them. I enroll in a community college, in our community college, the first college in the state that the African American became a president of the college Mr Zachariah could not be for more example. Where my problem come from was unknown to me in that school. I could not point to school, neither I can point to my job place resulting in reducing in my work load of forty hours a week, or my house I rented. There I met a lady call Maria, she was in her twenty's and I was in my thirty's, in all of my other girl friends she is the one that really confuse me, come she can not come, I want to be your friend, I will be thinking about it, I will have to tell my grandmother, and until the whole world knows about it, It will be impossible, we all humans, Case close.

A **society**, or a **human society**, is a group of people related to each other through persistent relations, or a large social grouping sharing the same geographical or virtual territory, subject to the same political authority and dominant cultural expectations. Human societies are characterized by patterns of relationships (social relation) between individuals who share a distinctive culture and institutions; a given society may be described as the sum total of such relationships among its constituent members. In the social sciences, a larger society often evinces stratification and/or dominance patterns in subgroups.

Insofar as it is collaborative, a society can enable its members to benefit in ways that would not otherwise be possible on an individual basis; both individual and social (common) benefits can thus be distinguished, or in many cases found to overlap. A society can also consist of like-minded people governed by their own norms and values within a dominant, larger society. This is sometimes referred to as a subculture, a term used extensively within criminology.

More broadly, a society may be described as an economic, social, or industrial infrastructure, made up of a varied collection of individuals. Members of a society may be from different ethnic groups. A society can be a particular ethnic group, a nation state, or a broader cultural group, such as a western society. The word *society* may also refer to an organize voluntary association of people for religious, benevolent, cultural, scientific, political, patriotic, or other purposes. A "society" may even, though more by means of metaphor, refer to a society organism such as colonial or any cooperative aggregate such as, for example, in some formulations of artificial intelligent.

Why we need to defined the society, Society make good thing happen in the country also make bad things happen among the people. They plan and execute their opinion.

Many people were kill in the war time, and shame in the war process, but after the war then there is a chance to being together as one country again. The blood shed will have to be remember for many years. The rebels was unconditional surrender to the federal government when they ran out of the ammunition and been kill like animals everyday, the action is call to surrender to the federal government was initiated by the rebels leader and carry out by his officers. The rebels leader flew to other neighboring country he was never c ought to surrender, he ran out from the country where he was fighting for his believe and to the outside of the country.

After many years of civil war, it was later forgiven by the present president. The civil war destroyed so many things that not only kill people but destroy most of the agriculture resources and the cattle's and crops that would have support the rebels. In fact at first the rebel gain the upper hand but when everybody see that their war was not justify including me can see that it is a fatal mistakes for the rebels to take the war action that way, then they started loosing power to the federal because there is no support for them and the federal gain more power by boosting more support and destroy the rebels. It was astonishing war, people celebrate and re-joys, we those that do not go to war were been to every day to be caution about their movement because small thing they see on the ground can result in a bomb and it can kill. The warning sending an alarm to be careful of any thing rebel army can plan to kill people and not to take for granted, these cause alarm for the federal that in the farm, the farmers reduce the farm production and they aware of the war.

Reduce in farm commodity means their will be scarce in farm products. The people aware of this scarce products and reduce their consumption. I go out with friend a lot sometimes something I observe is that I always hear two voices in my ear, my mind will be telling me something and the other mind will be telling me another thing. I never have one straight mind to began with, I believe that is good and evil, but what I sure of is one mind is right and the other is wrong. When I was a young boy, my character sometimes make me mad nd I have know idea of what is happening to me. Sometimes when I have a short sleep and short dream in the afternoon and when I woke up, I always woke up with my mind been shaking like some one that have all this world problems. I should have known all these in my young age or to take notice, I did not tell my parents neither my elder brother bit is something I am willing to do something about it on my own, but now what people think about me is that I don't know anything, I don't know my left from my wright. No wonder, I know, only God know how the people of Africa think and do their things, In the olden days of some parts of

Nigeria revealed that when woman have twin or born twins they usually sacrifice one of then by killing one and left one, and not until when the church missionary mission Mary S lessor arrived and stop the killing of children. I could not say more that the thinking and behavior of the African people is still today, believe in anything, not analyzing the situation very well before taken action. In my childhood, In the town I was born, I fear pet mostly dog. As I was standing with my parent, this dog come from nowhere and bite me in the leg, I cry and shout the dog, the dog, and the dog ran away. As a persistent, abnormal or irrational fear of animals, in-fact most pet related fear can be trace to traumatic experience an individual had with a particular animal. Some suffering from the effects of zoo phobia may have no traceable cause and would be classified as a phobia. The best way to prevent fear of pets from developing is by taking a proactive approach with the child at an early age, usually between the age of 4 to 6 and to teach them that animals are fun, friendly and safe for some people but for the pet you see outside, you must be careful, they are dangerous perhaps the dog lost his owner and left out to the street, and they are wondering all around, such as dogs or cats, they can bite you at anytime when they hungry, but for the house pet you train by your self will be a gentle touch. To achieved this self confident with the animals is by providing the girl or boy with a soft teddy bear to cuddle with or other books that they can read and get familiar with the pet and friendly, it can be helpful in teaching young children that pets are nothing to fear. Ignoring pet-related fear will not help and the child may not grow out of it overtime the fear gets worse with age. There are plenty of adults and senior who's fear of animals can be directly linked to a frightening experience they had during childhood.

We had a pet in our home a cat but we have no dog. Sometimes we fear that dog is a big animal that someone can own as pet, of cause today many people own different type of animal as a pet. It does not matter how big the pet it might be, good for them and they go along just fine. You can get ride of your pet if he do something stupid to you as a owner at all time, if your pet is stupid to you, you will kill the pet and eat it do you not or would you release the pet back to the wild untouched! Because the question puzzle me but I did not get a reasonable answer for my question. Anyway as I was saying, if a child appears to be having difficulty recovering an adverse experience, parents may help prevent fears from growing by providing rewarding, happy and safe experiences with animals. It is only a child that will not be able to differentiate between herbs and vegetable, the different can be notice from the vegetable that vegetable is a food but a herbs is a medicine, it was use to cure the sickness. Anytime my mother was not at home, it will be my responsibility to take care of my sisters and my brothers till my mother return, we feel secure with my father, but my father always busy receive stranger all the time, so he does not have much time to pay attention to us. In our little town, if I did not go out with my father I will go and see any festival was going on in the town. My father is an honorable man, he did not participate in any strange culture, and he did not allow anybody to talk him into any strange dialogue. here is story of my father in our town.

Every good story has a hero. In the matter of my father life and his death, Imam Azeez Sanni. Our hero name is Lasisi Sanni. As a chief imam of Okemagba he worked and organized with many towns combined together to make one. So he also strive to United and Unified many people by encouraging them to become a Muslim, doing the teaching and explaining what is Islam is all about in Islamic way. The Islamic way contain the rule and regulation of Islam, the law. after many years as a chief Imam he was disturb at what he considered as Kaferi. The Egungun and Oro people. Given the observation of the human mind no one can say for sure that Imam Azeez was not depressed by his action and what his philosophy was base on. By the same token it was Unequally presumptuous to say he was given the equivocal observation of friends and colleagues according to the Muslim religion and traditional way of living. The politics of the people at that time was very rough in that people they do not think very well and verbally about any one that try to make a difference. You neither follow what they believe or face the consequences, but regardless to the Imam Azeez there should be nothing to worry about even though he have different opinion that could cause the down fall of a party that should not be the case but to quiet in what he believed and without the other party explanation why he want the vote and what effort did he make.

For the policy's of the Imam Abdul Azeez and his supporter is too strong to believed in such a way that the Egungun, the masquerade people could be having a controversy with chief Imam. They should be doing their own thing as he should also be doing his own thing, nothing should be coming between them. During the Egungun festival, stopping at the front of chief imam house wishing him any thing will not be appropriate when they knew that they are not friends. Some people are stupid and ignorance, for the Egungun they should read the Qur'an and see what it said before trying to be friend with some one and to get the police to arrest them you will have to go several mile to make a report and there is no phone and no light in the town. The people of the time are not thinking. Some of my friends ask me that do you think the idea and the philosophy of the chief Imam Azeez could be brought back to the people of Okemagba, I said sure, nothing is impossible, with the help of God. God made it happen and give knowledge and the wisdom. God can do anything because it is too good to be truth. The notion that no one can say all standard are gone and so there are nobody left to do better than the chief Imam Lasisi is wrong. straight forward for a man, assume that man want every thing from woman. for the animal life style that they never think, they do the same thing over and over again without realize that they do made mistake and they should not do that again. But for human, this is a different case, human do reason and try to make adjustment where it necessary, so they will not make that kind of mistake again.

In our town, I will stand among people to watch what ever going on in the town where people were gather together watching. On one day I was surprise to witness a horror bothers that was fighting among themselves, I saw that day that a son can be fighting his step father because of a belief that he will be free from his step father after the fight. I don't know if the fight is not deliberately deliver for them because how could a father, a son, they are two against one with a long stick cane in their hands fighting each other. I never understand that kind of fight until they are tired of fighting and to beat each other with stick anymore. On the other hand I believed they are fighting about a particular culture which happen to be their culture, perhaps they are somebody else, but I called them stick boys. How could somebody enjoy beating him selves to hell with long stick in their hand and beating each other without they themselves realize it. They are older than me so I could not able to ask them why are they fighting that way, all their body is full of stick mark. After the fight they will have to go for treatment as I see I. Before I left my birth place, many crime were committed but there are no murderer or killings, the crime such as looters, destroyer, fighting among themselves and stolen their property and much more. After I evaluate this town, I hate their guts as I hate the killers. Too many deaths occurs in a year, they call it natural death, the hospital could not help them, even they go to the hospital for treatment they are illiterate, they know my father as a true teller (qualia), he always tell them the truth when it come to him, so they don't want to mess with someone that will leak their secret, even if they run from the scare crow or any other superstitious sign for that matter they were scare of supernatural but they do not believe in God, they may be going to church or mosque every time but they never listen to what the church or mosque was preaching about. My birth place was a cool place that they have a black swamp that run through town, and they go their and fish from the tropical water when they have time to go and fish, Any town that has no natural resources to live on, it will be difficult for a town to survive. The big city started from little town but because of river nearby and the road to transport back and fourth and or natural resources they have, the little town might developed and become a city, soon it will become a state on his own, so no doubt that when people can see something doing in a place like this people will rush in to take the advantages of the place. The black swamp is not much in support of anything except local people, they can only fish what they need, for many years, I never see the water change in color, because of its location or what have you but I also wonder if the black water really do exist from anywhere. I was curious at first to see a strange things, but really there is nothing strange about it that can surprise me.

So long for this town, a kid will always be a kids, when you come out from a good home, dad and mum give you a proper lesson, but something else coming to a brain that say how did you become something else again. We did not bring anything to this world, and at the same time we will not carry anything back when we die. As a kid, Some time you will need to play the house with your friends, doing nonsense thing without realizing that you are doing it. As a stupid kid, having sex with your brothers and sisters or any relatives in the house is a wrong thing to do. You are not from a gay family, your parent against this culture, but how do you and your brothers have to go out without your parent knowledge having sex or roman's at each other which is the opposite sex. A good kids will be able to explain what happens when things go wrong like that. They did not think, or aware what they are doing. Your parent believe in husband and a wife and it must be at some certain age and level before try to attempt the sexuality issue.

Marriage is not a simple thing in some society while the others society did not take it seriously as such. The couples will have children or expecting children on the way before they could agree to each other to be marry to themselves because they believe with the children between them, otherwise the marriage will not hold. In some other culture, they believe in for better for worse, they will marry each other anyway, but they expected children and their grandchildren. They gay couple, and bisexual society also dealt with their issue of marriage to each other, but does it really wise for one culture to impose its culture to others. It is like crushing on another when you know definitely that they are totally different entity.

We must recognized each other as civilized society and know how to deal with each issues. Having an idea of one society over the others and proving the superiority over others may not resolve any issues among them, but to recognized each other and have a respect to each other may be the best idea to resolve the issues in our society.

CHAPTER TWO

Cheaters

They say cheater will never proper, that is olden days, today cheater can prosper but how do we protect ourselves from the cheater, the people always want to cheat you of any kind but you must try to protect yourself, this type of idea is common in a poor country not in a developed country such as America. However, some people would like to take advantages of you and take a way what you rely on. In a poor country the people were so poor that they do not know God. Consider these example:

When I came back from the United State Of America to visit Nigeria in the year 2000. My junior sister called me and said my brother why don't you buy a piece of land right here in Lagos and have it build little by little as you can build it so that we can be seen each other and our family at all time, and I think is a good idea. I said to her that are sure of what you are saying about the land in Lagos because too many fraud about the land in Lagos, it is dangerous to buy a piece of land in

Lagos without a controversial that I have already deal with my brother in-law that told me the same thing that I can buy a house through a government program and we put money in it but nothing come out of it, no money back and no house. So I warned her about that, she said, she sure, I provide money to pay for the land which cost total of N170,000.00. The money was paid twice to the owner of the land and gave us receipt.

Then I make a foundation on the land and started building the house, all of a sudden there was another man called himself alhaji just came with police saying we can not build anything on the land because the person that sold the land does not have a right to sell us a land. The police take us to the police station and I made a statement with the police that was in the year 2000. The police told me to produce the evidence that I bought the land, I showed them the receipt from the man that sold us the land, the address of the man and his phone number, but instead of arrested him why he sold the land to us, the police insisted to go and arrest him, but arresting us. I came back from the police station when they get my bail out and I went to the man that sold me a piece of land that I was arrested because of the land that you sold to me and that you not supposed to sell the land. Then the man was so annoyed, saying why the police did not come to arrest him in his house that he was not a full right owner to sell the land, that he will not go to police station with us for any questioning after all he is right here. When I later go see the alhaji at his home and he demanded that we paid him; that the other party did not give him anything about the land, we paid the man another N50,000.00 and gave us receipt.

On till now this is how the land gang was causing the trouble all around the city and for the country trying to get the owner property that was not belong to them and up till now the police did not give me any feed back that I should go back and continue building my house, and my sister was later died after that year. It is has been a great and exciting phenomenal just to have a place call home and to have a base.

Further more the cheater want the money or property that is not belong to them, they will not mind if they will kill for it. What will happen when someone that do not have weapon go steal from someone that have a weapon it can only result in kill. The cheater will cheat anybody, white, black, yellow, or brown, young and old without remember tomorrow. The cheater will cheat you of anything not to talk of common woman, when woman cheat her husband you know that is out of joke, the love is not there any more, when there is no love between men and women that kind of thing can happen and if there are not religious in believing in the same ideology that adultery and fornication is not good according to the religion specification. Woman can also be a cheater in many way, they find way to entice men to give up or seduce him in a variety of ways. The woman cheater will look for a man to seduce and cheat him. Cheaters are bad people, they do not believe in God and some just do it for fun and for some they have determination that I will cheat somebody. Cheating does not concern with training someone or to be boss, cheating is a common idea that invested in humans, but when you join a gang then you may have boss and seniors. They can cheat anybody, even their relatives once it become their hobby. Cheater can never be prosper, who can say that he is responsible for the case of cheater (none) no case, cheater will never go out of his house except looking for someone to come by and be cheated, so he can start to deceived him and cheat him. Cheater will be walking around without specific goals in mind except who is going to be cheat and dump him as if he is nothing.

The cheaters are the once that look good that you can trust them of anything, is the cheater genuinely sorry for having hurt you and for having betrayed your trust! If you've been with this person long enough, you should be able to tell weather or not the cheater is sincere when he or she tells you they are sorry for what they have done, or weather the cheater is merely sorry he or she got caught, there's big difference. The cheater should be truly filled with remorse for his or her behavior. Some people jealously about the other people, I always pray for a miracle but not to the extend of cheating the others for a miracle to happen. Do you ever wonder why when you see a woman that you know that there is nothing that will come between you and her but because of the dress, the way she look, she always camouflage to you and many woman do that purposely to show her beauty.

A cheater can use many way to cheat you and let you down, the false miracle is miracle that get you nowhere, you dream but by the time you wake up you have completely forget about it. You couldn't remember if you are expecting something or not you see yourself, just get up in the morning you know exactly what you want to do and you go ahead and do it, such as you know you need to go to school in the morning after that you try and do your home work then perhaps you need to go to work for a part time job, then by the time you finished with all these you are already occupied. There are no time to trace your miracle. Another way of knowing false miracle is for someone betraying you all the time or promising you and never to fulfill the promises, the woman dress occasionally in a way that will look more attractive to men, appealing to the opposite sex that perhaps she is a model advertizing something or herself.

My dressing when I'm going out usually the same. I dress in formal way, that the way folk dress, but other time I prefer to dress informal way. I could not understand that kind of my behavior that I can not make up my mind with the way I am going to dress and look, feel, outside. My father was rich in his own time but not to that extend. Formal way of dressing is to dress expensively with new cloths, new shoes, and the cloth will be expensive rather than just any cloth. I think perhaps this was an act of shy, I was shy with the people but should I shy!, I was not dating any woman and sometime I never see any of my girl friend in town for some days unless we meet at school, and all of them are secret lovers that I never express my feelings to them publicly. We play at school play ground, we dance, and we eat and do our home work that is all, nothing much in between us but why shy. You know what!, I call it stupidity because I do not know that I was shy to a girl in my age at my birth place. I fear my father because I was too young to be having girl friends but nobody was saying anything about it, then why shy!, I know some typical household that they hold nothing back between them and their children up to the sex education, they show their children how they should be with woman and to behave, so no wonder some of them fear no woman to have sex with a girl and as time goes on they can not deal with their marital statues, they end up in the divorce. Many of those boys and girls, they were also have their children in a wedlock, they have no plan for their marriage not to talk of their child and their child end up also in no hope for the future. The sex education is good simply my friends want to ride an expensive car and dress expensively, the sex education tell you why you should have a sex with woman or man, save sex and at what age but not only to know how to ejaculate with woman, but it can later result in a wedlock.

At my birth place as I was saying, there are no murderer but a lot of crime were committed such as burglary, house burnt down, and sometimes argument result in a fight that the head of the ruler in the town will have to settle the case for them. There was a time that the stealing in the town was anonymous and worse that they couldn't catch the thief before the sunrise, the thief steal every property in the town such as gold, cloths, money, and other things they can find and fleet the town before morning. They stole from door to door, house to house and the funny things is that they can't be caught so the Otunba the head of the town ruler get themselves together to find solution to the problem and what they come out with is to hire a night watchman that will be looking for the thief and watching the peoples properties after they gone to sleep. It sound like a plan, but can they caught the thief?.

Further more, Otunba the head of the rulers in the town sound the bell that every residence of the town should be present in front of his palace, and everybody do so as he said, he said the thief problem at hand know is to hire a night watchman that will guide the town at night so that every body can sleep without worrying that thief is coming to come and steal their properties. All the resident said it is a good idea, they accept the advice he brought up, and he later told them how much each house will be paying every month until they have no more night watchman or more stealing in the town. The rule for having watchman is that as from 10.00pm to 5.00am there should be nobody on the street of our town otherwise he will be stop and questioning because the night watchman will be outside at that hour looking for trace-pass.

In fact the people of the town can do these job by themselves isn't it, by protecting themselves but the problem is that they will forget not to fall asleep in the night, and when they do the thief have a chance to come in to any house and steal more of their things. When the night watchman resume their duty, you can hear them by blowing their whistle every minute and some people wake up during the time they catch the people that trace-pass that what is going on out there. They will blown their whistle and started to questioning the trace-passer, that do they not hear when the ruler of the town make the law or why are they disobeying the law of the town, If the trace-passer have good explanation that he was coming from somewhere important and that is why he or she was out late, the night watchman will let him or her go, but if she refuse to have a good explanation he or she will be reported to the head of the ruler of the town and can now be summon why he or she disobeying the law of the town.

For some month things are quiet in the town, no more stealing and no more burglarize. The night watchman get paid through the people of the town contribution, each household have to paid some certain amount of money every month to paid off the night watchmen including our house, off-cause the ruler of the town can not afford the night watchman salary by himself because the government is not paying them then, so then, he will need more contribution from the people of the town especially rich people like my father can give him money at anytime. The idea seems to be a happiness to the people of the town, the ruler of our town have done his job at that time, and they find a way to protect his people from the danger of been fear burglarize. No government intervention involved not until now that the government have to know about what is going on each town of our country. To be improvise is for the ruler of the town not to take any action when things are going wrong in the town, but to correct the problem and bring every one into the order, every man must provide for his own household and care for the people of the town.

During the time of politics and chaos, the head of the rulers Otunba and Bale of the town must know how to deal with the town problems both psychological and physiologically they must dealt with the problem and provide solution and relief if possible to the people of the town. It is a great mistake sometime to see both Otunba and Bale the chiefs of the town to be fighting each other over a duty of the town, sometime otunba himself can be a victim of the people of the town in a political time some how the situation must be ratify by the government because nobody else say you right or wrong otherwise the situation will remain worse. In early 60s and 70s the political situation make the town scatter, divided into many segment of life that some people refused to listen to the chief and the rulers of our town and to avoid the collision of the town with the missionaries and the outsider, the chief call every household member in the town to his quarters and ask them that he needs their support and to be united so that the town transition will go smoothly. In the case of our chief Imam lasisi that is my dad, the destruction of his property and his death was not happen without all the situation arises from the town. The Otunba of the town allowed the outsider that mean the person that was not born in that town to be molesting the people of the town and with the town situation off-cause when we are one country, both church missionary and the outsider can cause much trouble and damage to the people of the town, consider the burglary robbery situation that has been going on for so long in the town that the chiefs and rulers of the town can not figure out that the problem have been laid down for them, without knowing why is happening and who is doing it, they forget that without the thief inside nobody know how your house is organized.

My father, as a head of his own household have his own moral and obligation to his household and to the people of the town he represent. He was also a family member to the head of the rulers of our town called Otunba. Sometimes they are not as friendly as they do not agree with each other philosophy sometimes, so they are not much that friendly. However, because of the work at my father's hand, God work, it make him to forgive his enemy.

Now the problem I see is not from human being is from God, and the problem is when you can not explain what really happen in the past in full details then how do we know whom to blame, we can not afford ourselves just been annoyed at all time without knowing what really causing the madness. Perhaps they have no history written down or lack of knowledge, they are the worse race I ever seen, is like a child that can not talk, how do we know how to treat the child. If you are stranger and you arrived at a town at the time of political turmoil in the country, and you did not recognized it, a lot of people may confuse about it, the victimized and the victims want the way to revenge about their situations, and what ever you carry away with, will be a blessing to you when you can not flip it around.

There are many ways a cheater can cheat, actually cheating refers to immoral way of achieving a goal. It is generally used for the breaking of rules to gain advantages in a competitive situation. Such as codes from an unwritten code of conduct based on morality. Ethics or custom, making the identification of cheating a subjective process. Cheating can refer specifically to marital infidelity. Someone who is known for cheating is referred to as a cheater in other language.

The academic cheating is an extremely common among high school and colleges in around the world. If to say no cheating less students will be able to pass their exams paper. The new revolution in high-tech digital info contributes enormously to the new way in cheating, online term-paper even in the classroom the student do cheat the examiner sometime if too many student were in the class. They cheat from what they have jot down in the rough paper from home, and nowadays technology; the people cheat through someone that knows the subject well staying outside with his laptop and begin to signal to the other customer in-side transmitting the correct answer to him or her.

In many culture couples expect sexuality from each other and the cheating is commonly refers to infidelity, such as adultery and adulterer, touching and talking may also be equally damaging to other peoples culture and cheating can be term as abuse to the others. With the expansion of understanding of other cultures there is a wide spectrum of what cheating means. Cheating constitutes to when in relationship, the definition of cheating is based on both men and women and how they defined their marriages and their understanding high or lower of this definition.

Sport are govern by rules and the acts that forbidden it, by sport commission at the event. Forbidden act include use of drug, performance enhancing, and harassment or injury the competitors. Those rule can be consider as cheating when did not respect. sport, games, and gambling they can be easily cheated when playing it. One of the gambler I ever seen said no one cheated them, the poker gambling, they want to be cheated, even though he has a secret code or smart and know how to play it, people will said is cheating them because he wins all the time. Truly speaking there is concern that this is not truly cheating, as it is the fault with the machine in the first place, However as with the live sports, it is cheating if the player is not playing the game in approved manner. As in sport and games, cheating in gambling is generally related to directly breaking rules or laws; or misrepresenting the event being wagered on, or interfering in the outcome. A boxer who takes a dive, a casino which plays with secretly loaded dice, a rigged roulette wheel or slot machine, or a doctored deck of cards, are generally regarded as cheating, because it has misrepresented the likelihood of the game's outcomes beyond what is reasonable to expect a better to protect himself against.

How do you describe your success story in life as unfold. Some people describe themselves as unthinkable that means no plan was so ever made but most company's today plans ahead of time in other to pay off their debts and to balance their budget. Most of the CEO in 2000 fortune company's and most of the new born, happen to be a woman or man, he or she attributes his or success to persistence, learning from mistakes and surrounding himself with great people. To describe your success, we know that fast growing business like your company have needs to increase in your business or to get more customer and to move your business forward in any number of ways and that if you did not plan for the new ways and the technology that can help you achieve your goals the situation will be left unsolved.

It make sense that more than 20 percent of Inc. 500 companies this year are either marketing firms or government contractors. The past decades has been about connecting and protecting and fulfilling the needs of gadget and other companies beyond those categories other company's cluster speak to state of guarded, discrimination, dread and the racial slot are the game changing media business. Unlike radio, television stations and the internet that contract with social media and promote the business may have a negative effect in the image that was been pursuit. The society and the organization have never care about anybody, what the people want is to work and get their pay check and their benefits, as the government intervention the companies, so as the society getting better off, because more benefits will be available; more jobs will be created; and also more benefits to the employee, such as increase in wages, hospital benefits, holidays benefits and much more.

The accountant and the managers are there to protect the Asset of a company not to go bankruptcy on aware. The crush of cyber security and identity thief protection firm and the falling of credit card protections were also affected. Through out the late 90s progress, the 2000 Inc. 500 company's did not appear to operate under a cloud of unusual risk, although many of those business soon suffered from declining to prevent these from happening, many of these firm have to cry to the government to provide the help neither by tax cut or some kind of leverage, now we are getting somewhere with the local government to provide security for the local firm and descend on the government as a way of keeping their contract long before it could expire, no wonder we can see such post as president, governor and other big executive ties to the company that deal business with them in other to survive their ordeal. The accusation behind the business that they can not prove as a case that is a tangible is regarded as a sin, sin is a something that can not be proving or call reality, one can't help feeling more guarded than watchful of how recent events will play out for this years, oil and real estate business. There's a reason for the crowding in the government services category, it bring stability to the organization. The government especially; the federal government and the state government are still an excellent customer, perhaps they were founded by the retired government employee and government officials. Most entrepreneurs off-cause view risk and then lack of choice, there is a risk and then recklessness in-valved, and companies on fast growth path must be especially careful not to wonder off the designated walkway.

The company could not even careless if the employee went blank without notice. More encouraging are the company's sprouting in industries such as carpet industries, floor and tiles, from the manufacturer to the whole sales and to the retail needs to be very careful, these sectors represent teeth-grinding tough issues on which entrepreneurial zeal and fresh thinking are surely needed not to mention those small organization security firm, auditor firms and much more that signal or will sign the contract with the big company. For example, The capet company as a whole sale company of Capet and rugs, they hire a security firm security firm to manage their security department as contractor and also they hire the Auditor firm from outside to manage their auditor department. They all benefits from the big company, what happen after is another thing, the company may still be standing as usual and still pumping their resource to their customer, the lesson are learned about their races and discrimination that have been causing them to loose profits and ravaging their products. The firm will do the right thing not you but security Guard that suppose to enjoy the benefit of it. Many employee were hire through small agency and sent to the big company to perform their job duty. The pay can be manage but the risk involve in that kind of situation is that why the employee goes blank without notice from the big company is because they belief that the employees are not working for them they are working for small agency that hire them and the employee will collect their pay check from where they were hired.

The carelessness of Mr. right and Mr. wrong can put the old idea into a jeopardy that the employee will be left with the small scale firm that they are, the small scale firm have no chance of paying any benefit to them, and be left for suffering till the rest of their life if no program was put in place. The act of the people and the confusion of power must be balance in modern day America that cripple the idea behind not given the proper information to the employee that they are to do their job and do it thoroughly as they suppose to do it and no expectation except what the company can offer them. The son in the heart land, you can hear it everywhere, on the radio, on the television, in the market, anywhere you can find advertisement, the show is always on. The market compete each other saying don't breath on me, don't be too smart, that we all know the fear game. Yes it's a game but you have to be smart about it, every tic tact that they can do to get their contract going; but what that does to you rather than protect you for that day and the rainy day. The security guard firm can not hold on many employee, so they hire and train as they need people, the sloppy employee, the sleeping on duty employee, and vagabond know that is not a place for them to growth; in that kind of environment because they may be terminated at anytime.

My advice on this topic is the case of my brother my father. Any relatives company can cause you much more than you think. They will like you to do much more for them and to help them as much as you can, I call that overweight, no one should play business deal with friends and family otherwise they will pull you down and ruins your business. Business time and leisure time are totally different time. After expressing what you feel and what you think; is time to turn the case back to you, no matter how you can prove yourself, it is there, perhaps who will blame himself later when the business started going down!, also up and down situation they descend on you to the point that they do not know how to talk business except to abuse you, but when it comes to them they will like to change the game play to favor them.

There are certain class of some people that undoubtedly feminine from their earliest youth, they have shown marked inclination for the habits and the dress of woman; and when they are adult they do everything in their power to obliterate their manhood. It is equally true that such non sex males will possess a strong attraction for some abnormal individual. But it is a common mistake to suppose that all the tribe betray these attributes. The majority differ in no detail of their outward appearance. Their physical or their dress from normal men. There are athletics, masculine in habits, truth in man, passing through society year after year without arousing his inner temperament.

As I said from the beginning of this chapter that woman are the big spender, woman like going out buying different king of things, It is their habit to spend their money on the household things and on the other hands, man like to buy an expensive thing to the house such as car and houses and so many other point. In a marriage they expect children and offspring from the family. If woman try to cheat his husband will be on jealousies; which means they probably jealous his husband by spending money on other woman. Woman spend money on grocery and some household items, in fact woman make money less than man but know most of the job is woman jobs. Since woman have join the labor market, woman have been making headway.

Another way cheating can occur is true the dream, I said this often and often, but don't take my word for it, I could remember that, sometimes when I woke up from my dream it seems I woke up to the car, that the engine of the car is already gone, sounding like the starter will not start or the engine will stop, all of sudden, my head become heavy burden, the chest ran to somewhere else, its a lonely dream until I woke up and realize that it is only a dream. Since the time I travel, I never sleep one day without dreaming both night and day, I know the other part of me never sleep in the night or in the day, running day and night, not to talk of my enemy that won't let me rest. Everyday and night running around in the car, factory, also at the place of work, where sometimes have to perform their ritual behaviors in the morning, in the middle of the night and so on. If you ask them why they are doing that they will say we will have something to tell you. It make you wonder.

Since investigation of moderate tolerance began it has become clear that they are a complex experience and part of a larger phenomenon now designated as altered state of consciousness, pathological conditions often predominate among the other types of tolerance state such as comas, cold syndrome, allergic syndrome and suspended remote animation. All these are associated with unconsciousness as are a member of other state resulting from certain drug or the effects of disease upon the body chemistry and these are all more intense than other altered states such as normal sleep, hypnoses, or to be bullish.

Of many types of altered states of consciousness, tolerance is among the most valuable for it's moderation, recognizing the moderation that the subjective realm of man's mind may be investigated, most conveniently, many people who have applied moderation have realized that in effect is a method for expanding awareness. There many state in which consciousness Is withdrawn from the normal waking level which collectively we may call fear states. Some can be created by hypnosis by drugs like mescaline and others can be entered by certain logic practices. A medium, or a sensitive, can pass voluntarily into one of these states, in which consciousness is withdrawn to an interim level of the self, and can at the same time maintain a communication line to the external world. Because it is the self induction of a trance state and is relatively free of pathological conditions, medium ship affords a greater element of control over the experience.

I was not a born psychic, but with a background of paranormal experience, neither my parent also had any knowledge of such matters, even after my enthusiasm, I didn't accept these developments without serious self question and intellectual analysis, I wanted to keep my experiences on as scientific a basis of possibility. As I began to have out of body experiences both at work and at home, I knew it, this is not a new thing to me, but my last experience with paranormal was still strange, at work and at home with Seth. We packed every table ware, we rearrange all the dishes plates and arrange them set by set, but it really happen that small sets, big sets,and other set should be in the formed of sets, and they all go out back for use in the form of first in first out. Anyway assume that Seth correctly described the job as correctly.

We all know what is set, set is a series of number, however a personalities as Seth; or call it a spirit possession; is dam good one, a daemon that directed to the abstract object has concern man kind through the ages. Though there is another way to deal with this extrasensory perceptions, I hope I can throw some light upon the nature of such experiences and to show that human personality has ability and other ways to receive knowledge than those it real concern. Moderation is a fascinating and provocative subject for it touches upon essential question about the mind of man, the nature of his consciousness, and even his ultimate destiny.

My parents are a brand new religion, the religion that was not of their forefather, but adopted to new one, was a sort of social protestation, rather delightfully innocent of dogmatism. In general, God loved everyone, boys and girls with starched shirts, acceptable to their reasonable services. Neither of us we children was bitter about a God's apparent injustices. We didn't pay too much attention to that because everyone know that, that will be time of thinness and the time of thickness. When you share the sweetness of it without a doubt, you will know that without that, their will be no implementation for the new things. Although each of us felt a strong sense of contact with nature, no one was more surprised than I was then, to find myself quite abruptly speaking about it and disappointed for what it suppose to be a straight forward believe.

I feel betray myself at times thinking that even my African forefather would have found spirit in the back yard rather than hard to take, sometimes I think he was superstitious, a surviving soul seemed part of the puzzles of adult no nonsense; but now I know that human personality has a far greater than moderation. Every-body that came to United State of America were all immigrants in one way or the other. To get employment is a difficult tax to pass-by. You must present your social security card number at the time of employment. The old folks that make the law may have forgotten that it will be a difficult situation to them at long run, some folk could have two card instead of one card social security in other to cheat the government. They have duplicate birth certificate or false one just to present for employment and other benefits they can get from the government. This is a smart thing to do from their point of view. The same thing is still happening today to the new immigrants that have no documentation to show to the government or to get a job. Then is that a cheating!.

I felt as knowledge was being implanted in the very cells of my body, so that I couldn't forget it a gut knowing, a biological spirituality. It was a feeling and knowing, rather than intellectual knowledge. At the same time I remember having a dream the night before which I had forgotten, in which this same sort of experience had occurred, every night that the night mare occur not during the day, it mean that dream have something to do with night and day, but behold, I have seen it from the long distance, and I knew the two were connected. Of cause, as a human being, my bleeding from noise and every part of my body occur when ever I was sleeping and dreaming at the same time. I know that the enemy will do everything to still and kill and destroyed. This time they don't even care if you are Muslims or Christian or Buddhism, living not living, you owed the slavery to them, or just roaming around the street and do what ever pleases you, the return is a guarantee. African society behave like they don't know anything, the old idea is still in them, if they cannot do something they should keep their mouth short. Send you back and forth without any clue, you know you must do it yourself when the government can not support you, you must support yourself and find the means to justify yourself. This happen from the most part of the world, the slave trade, the rise and fall of the African people and what happen, the experience have been forgotten. They will repeat the same thing over and over again. Moreover, to give the benefit of the doubt, they ask you to go get arodon which mean something that sweetening. They sent you to go and collect it from somewhere and bring it back, they knew that you can not find what you are looking for, but is that the way to express something like this, they call it idiom language. The system that can never work; that was saturated; because they were never think deeply enough about the future, and that is why they borrow culture from culture to culture.

The ideas that I received it were just as starting, however, I just didn't know that everything had its own purpose. Now I suddenly felt the fantastic vitality present even in things I would previously considered insanity. A nail was sticking to the wall and I experience ever so briefly the consciousness of the atoms and molecules that compose it. They turned all the idea of reality upside down, we know that what ever we practice; we could be good at it, but have you try and make the research and see how good your idea is! good or bad, you can not rely on your idea alone; ask second opinion and get the full picture not half picture. We rely on our physical being, what we made; support us in our economy and our military, also arouse our brain. As it was, I didn't know what had happened, yet even then I felt that my life had suddenly changed. The word revelation came to mind and I tried to dismiss it, yet the word was critical. I was simply afraid of term with its mystical implication, both knowing and unknowing. I was familiar with inspiration in my own soul, by this, I was as different from ordinary inspiration, I knew I was been forcing into another dimension which is another religion that could say only the night I can have a dream. Manipulating the situation around me. Taking the advantage of the situations

The gift from God is a blessing, everyone pray everyday for miracle to happen. They ask god to give them good life, good health, and good children that will listen to them when they get old. But humans forget that the present individual in any given life could be called a given moment. Having all the properties of original entity, the image that you saw was a personality moment of his own, it contains all the abilities of you but not to say it was permanent of person for special purpose. This type of personality moment is of different origin that you who is himself of his own entity. The close encounter is sometimes so dramatic that it amounts to a religious experience which can form the basis for a spiritual movement. Such encounters frequently transform the witness's personality and outlook, causing them typically to become more creative, open to new ideas, sensitive, psychically aware and especially spiritual in fact and outlook where the unconscious plays a greater part in daily life in a more ways.

Although such psychic expressions are usually thought of as all in the mind, it is clear that this part of the mind is conjunction with altered states of body can actually manipulate physical reality. Under certain conditions it will use this ability to produce realities with a temporary upgrade physical aspect. That make those who see them absolutely convinced that they really exist. The close encounter or any other form of physical manipulation bring the precisely this order of perceptions that brings into question the relationship between our minds and what we conventionally call reality. The reality status of dreams or even hallucinations is not always enough for the unconscious, it wants to become externalized in a way that dreams do not satisfy. Nor does it only settle for the identity of an extraterrestrial. There was an allusion to their strange physical aspects or that they display. From a common point of view one would be entitled to argue that either something is physical or it is not, and surely there is no selectivity or strangeness about the issue. However, this physicals is not just out there but is is apprehended by the witness perceptual system. The unconscious by duplicating such subjective perceptions, can convince the witness of their concrete nature. These are the processes at work in the unconscious staging of physical being and their object, that you need to look for something indestructible to come alive.

Numerous experiments with seed has been found where their growth is monitored have taken place. Those exposed to psychic influence have been found to have developed faster than control seeds without such exposure. Microscopic examination has detected changes in the cell protoplasm associated with the enhanced growth. Not only on seed or any other animals that the experiment have been taken place, it is in every creature on earth is been carried out. The seed treated by the healer showed a higher yield than the untreated, the result of which undoubtedly indicate that the human system can manipulate physical reality selectively, and the implications of this must be numerous.

Some people think that we are stuck in physical reality like flies, so that each motion we make only worsens our predicament and hastens our extinction. Others see the universe as a sort of theater into which we are thrust as birth and from which we depart forever at death. Open your eyes and see, we do not need to take a big mount out of a mount hills, every thing we see appear to us as we see it, physical form in humans dimension. In fact any other dimensions may exist in this world or any other part of the universe, but the world we lived in suggest that when we die the soul go away, where he goes was unknown. Judgment after life was also unknown because nobody die and come back to life again. Our physical creation may die and come back alive again because we create them, to the extend that if someone create human being and other creations that was alive in this world, the belief that the creator will be alive and well and can make judgment and total empowerment over humans and all of his creations is not a doubt. So, in our physical world, what we see is what we believed, we see our-self, we see the other creations and we try to imitate what God create or what we humans think God's said.

We can not be alone in the universe, unless God make his image in form of human being or his other creation. When we sleep, we see know one, our soul go far away as he could possibly go, but when we woke up the soul remember to come back, but when we die, the soul never come back again, It wonder away without recall. The ghost, the psychic, monster and other aspect of our life are all trying to cheat us, cheat us of our life, the gain we achieved in life, such as savings, obedient to Gods, knowledge, and other material valuable objects. Humans have conker the world long time a go and realize that know one else can hide somewhere except humans that have something to hide.

Many people of course feel that death is new beginning, but most of us still think that we are formed and bound by our physical bodies and environment. Many who believe in an afterlife think that current event s are thrust upon us indiscriminately, still others believe that good or bad events are sent to us as rewards or punishments. But most people take it for granted that we are pretty much at the mercy of events over which we have little control. The chemicals themselves will not give rise to consciousness or life, consciousness comes first and evolves it own form. All the cells in the body have a separate consciousness, there is a conscious cooperation between the cells in all the organs and between the organs themselves. Molecules and atoms and even smaller particles have a condensed consciousness, they form into cells and form an individual cellular capable of much more experience and fulfillment that would be possible for the isolated atom or molecule alone. This go on to form the physical body mechanism even the lowest particle retains it individuals and it abilities through this cooperation are multiplied a million-fold.

Physical matter makes consciousness effective within three dimensional reality. As individualized energy approaches your particular field it expresses itself to the best of its ability within it. As energy approached, it creates matter; first of all in an almost plastic fashion. But the creation is continuous like a beam or endless series of beams, at first weak as they are far off, then stronger; then weak again as they pass away. Matter of itself, however is no more continuous, not more given to growth or age that is, say the color.

No particular object exist long enough as an indivisible, rigid, or identical thing to change with age. The energy behind it weakens. The physical pattern therefore blurs. After a certain point each recreation becomes less perfect from your standpoint. After many such recreations that have been unperceived by you, then you notice a difference and assume that a change has occurred. The actual material that seems to make up the object has completely disappeared many times, and the pattern has been completely filled again with new matter. There is no more truth and no more falsehood in saying that my appearance in the doorway was caused by suggestion than to say that this room and everything in it is caused by suggestion. You will understand that it is erroneous to think in terms of one physical universe. When we tear apart of our body by doing master-bat-ion you are doing yourself a favor that is going to affect you for long time. You now exist in four different ones at this moment.

The house was the focus for a number of identifiable field effects. A magnetic field can cause household objects to move, causing poltergeist like noises. It can also set up vibrations in the inner ear and in the structural materials of the walls, roof, etc. An electrical field can energize circuitry intensity causing thermal effects due to shorting and create localized burning of the wiring. The smell like burning rubber can be created by predictable electrical discharges in the air, such discharges change the energy states of various atoms and numerous chemical compounds can be formed. It has been mentioned that nitrogen making up 70% of the air, changes to a metastable state.

Can we cheat death!, It was known that some people cheat death. But in my own view no body can cheat death, when the time is complete to die, there is no way around it. In some cases, the cheating can occur through the materialistic things. The treasure that was bury with the death and later discovered by living may account for cheating, but at any rate, some people think is a treasure. It would seem that the electrical emitted by people acts as a carrier wave for psychic effects, psychics are bound up with the phenomena that occurs around them. There comes a point in these people's lives when they are triggered to produce these things. The trigger can be field effects, radio waves, especially radar, proximity to lighting strikes, or pr-thunderstorm, whether they are affected or not would depend on the type of field mixture involved. Its a strength and the particular wavelength to which the witness is hypersensitive. The same basic issue is that the people also invariably have some degree of food and chemical allergy, they are often characterize as being unwell on a more or less permanent basis and untreated allergies can go unrecognized for years and become progressively worse until the suffer is put on a specialized diet.

Do we know anything about the tongue!, many people can believe that many things goes through the tongue. But the most dedicates part of our body is how we eat and what we eat. It's good to eat right by eating a proper diet. We can prolong the life expectancy. Eating unhealthy food will not gives us proper stamina. To be in a good stamina means we are balance in our immune system. The tongue is carefully place the food to our mouth and go to our stomach through the esophagus, if the food is too hot, the tongue will know, if it is too cold, the tongue will also know. So, we know what we eat, and it will definitely go through our digest system and come out as a waist. Since is not part of our body, it will definitely not staying there, such as tablets that we use when we sick, medicines and other unwanted food we mistakenly eat.

There they come, they come by car, by horse, no humans no cry. The harder they come the easier they fall. They come to gossip like the Indian movies that show gust that they must surround with their bowls and arrows like olden day movies and they throw fire into the houses, wake them up from their sleep while they make them dream at night. The terrible guilt that allow the cheater to live the horrible life style. The cheater at night cheat you through the consciousness, split your conscious mind into two dimension and make you dream. Cheater cheat anytime, no weapon is greater than what cheaters has because they do just about anything to cheat you.

When you believe in two religion such as Christianity and the Muslim, and you practice both religion and you know that the spiritual of the two way were different from each other. Which one is superior and which one is not then you are the most objective mediums I have ever known. If people believed in reincarnate, also it may be true or not most religion suggest that there is reincarnation after life, but nobody really know what happen next when they die. No death to stay withing physical reality. This is only to show you what was possible, and to bring you both male or female to an understanding of inner reality. Everybody chose his death, It was not thrust upon us. We did not manufacture sufficient blood, for he did not want to be physical beyond the time he had allotted. He wanted to give you an impetus, and his effect was far stronger than had he lived, and he knew this. He had a horror of living to young male-hood for he did not want to meet a young woman, become attracted and continue with another physical life. He was a light to you and the light is not extinguished. It will lead you into knowledge that you would not have known otherwise. All this story about reincarnation is not my story, I do believe however that there is a God, the creator, so possibly life after death when we will give the account of what we have done in our life time. Repeating the same pattern of life could not make sense. I will not wast my time about this reincarnation stuff. Most of the book I read myself to support my proof did not yield any clue. So I recommend to you if you need to know more about the reincarnation you can go direct to the sources book.

I gave you several example about the world we live in and our universe in general. The cheater and the cheat, what was cheating us and who are the people that cheat the others. Everything is in our world. The religious leader also give several example not to cheat each other that everything in the universe is by order.

CHAPTER THREE

Security Guard

A security officer is a person who is paid to protect property, asset or people. Security guard usually privately and formally employed personnel. A contract between two parties. A services of one another under a contract to hire, often security officers are uniformed and act to protect property by maintaining a high visibility presence to deter illegal and intruders actions, observing directly through patrols, and by watching alarm systems, video cameras for the intruder, fire and other inappropriate actions, then the security will take an appropriate action and report the incident to their client and notify the security supervisor before calling police and the higher authority and other nearest government emergency agency. The emergency services organization ensure the public safety and their health by addressing different emergencies. Many agencies engage in community awareness and prevention danger and to help the public avoid danger, detect, and report emergencies effectively. Until recently, the term watchman was more commonly applied to this function. Night watchman also commonly use for the name in general, security is generally regarded as fulfilling a private policing function.

Many security firms and proprietary security departments practice to detect, deter, observe and to report. Sincerely speaking, security officers were not allow to make an arrest but have the authority to challenge, observe and take a necessary action by collecting the necessary information and to speak to visitor or intruder to leave the premisses gently.

The major economic justification personnel is that insurance companies such as fire insurance company give substantial rate discount to sites which have a 24 hours security presence for high risk. The discount often exceed the money been spent on its security program, discount offered because having security officer present with security effective tend to diminish the shrinkage that might have occurred inside company such as thief, misconduct, sabotage and much more.

Today security guard is must have in firm or apartment building at least to secure the site even though they do not carry guns just to observe and to detect the intruder and call the law enforcement. Those firm prefer to have someone watching rather than to leave the gate open with nobody there to check them in to the site, If the security guard suspect or see illegal weapon carrying into the building then the security guard will know what to do. If this approach is use encourage employee to meet outside of work in informal settings.

Nowadays that many things are changing and it changes for the better, there are different types of exams for a security to go through in today's security guard job such as CPO, certified protection officer. The benefits gained to the employer and the employee are immeasurable. For the employer the knowledge that they have and effective well trained and skilled, security force is another total experience that when needed will be able to respond to challenging situation with competence and professionalism. The employee gain the benefits of a higher level of training at low cost, confidence in his skills, the performance of his job, and an internationally recognized title to associated himself with.

The thing to stress is that the CPO designation is not just another requirement, it is a designation that they should be proud of. Make them aware of that, present it to them as something that they'll want to do, not something that they have to do. You will find that most people with a little encouragement will welcome the chance to obtain their CPO, but enough for the CPO, many company also hire a security officer that do not have the security officer knowledge, they will need to be train from the security firm that hire them, motivated and know what they suppose to do on the job.

The OBT program is ideal for a pr-assignment training, new orientation or basic training for the security officers that already on the job, this 16hours course is comprised of 8hours of entry level security officer training and 8hours of additional basic skills. This track covers a diversity of topics in a user-friendly format.

Introduction to duty and responsibilities, professional and ethics, reports writing, patrol techniques, legal concept and first aid basic, the employee must have some educational knowledge or a high school diploma for him or her to be able to write and read. Including skill that a security officer most know are (1) must be able to interact with public, (2) professionalism and ethics, (3) patrol and make round, (4) reports writing, (5) must know the legal authority and when to call police, (6) fire hazard detection and prevention, (7) procedure for safety, emergency and much more.

However for the professionalism, no one is perfect only god is perfect, but to follow the proper guidelines that was provided for you and follow it exactly the way they want you do it can be specify as professionalism along with it is the ethics, you must know about the people you are dealing with everyday and be able to provide and go along with their norm, so that you will not have too much hard time dealing with them. Both you and the people you deal with day to day must be able to render this idea.

A security guard must be able to interact with people, speak the language people are using and be able to give them a direction from the gate to the offices and if security is in the middle of the client, customer, a security guard must be watchful alert and challenge the intruder neither by sitting or standing. When a security guard make patrol around the yard, inside the building, and by patrol car or by foot she must know how to read and write and speak in the language the people speak e.g English. Again a security guard must be able to give direction from the gate to the receptionist in the office and when paroling the yard and offices, the employee and visitor may ask the security guard a question, he must be able to answer the question.

How do you trust the security guard that he will not steal from the client, the answer to that question depends on how the security guard want his job, it is necessary to collect as much information as employer can from the employee so that something like that does happen he can be held responsible. The training will be provided to show the employee the reason why they hire them in the first place. A good employee will not attempt such incident.

Report writing and calling the police to the rescue if the intruder does happen, you must write in the language the people speak and to be able to speak to the police and any other law enforcement officer, because sometimes they themselves need to write their own report for their own case, in case the intruder need to be charge to the curt. Further more both law abiding citizen and intruder, the security guard need to speak to them in a polite way.

Now we come to analyze what can get a security officer fired from the line of duty. Lateness can get security officer fire, the visitor or the employee of the company complain against the security guard that is not doing his job properly, sleeping on duty, the security forget to make round and not call in when he suppose to call while is on duty. If the security officer involved in all this rules the employment will be terminated.

Fire hazard detention and prevention, some company's think that they need additional security is require for their firm such as ADT security and others. ADT have their electronic equipment install in the client building and ADT monitor the whole scene from their office. So both security guard and ADT must co-operate together to watch the site building. In any case that the security is there monitoring the building, if the intruder do occur during this time. The ADT will give a security guard a call, if the phone was picked up then they know he was there, and if no phone was pick up then they no that there is know security guard fall asleep. The ADT will send their representative to come and check the building, the trained security at security guard office will show the candidate how to use fire hazard in the case fire do happen and to prevent it from happening.

A security guard must be smart and can remember what happen for your memory. Everything in live growth through the sun, when you are born you never know any thing no matter how your memory is sharp it can only pick up the hereditary you inherit from your parents neither your father or mother but definitely we learn everything we met in the world. If we can be patient about everything when we fail about some issues or success you will eventually reach there and that is where some people are more excel than the others. Some people are slow in doing thing and while the people that have practice about he issues can dominate the particular issues. Focus and good judgment of character can help you to be a good security guard.

There are many field in security that can lead any one to a higher position.

There are different type of security today such as (1) private security (2) building security (3) corporate security (4) business security (5) event security (6) armed security (7)retail security (8)private investigations (9) undercover. Some security guard carry gun to protect where they assign them from their office. Armed security and unarmed security.

The armed security guard such as bank security guard, armored car security guard, building security guard they collect the money from the retail store to the bank, they carry gun stick to protect themselves. All these security guard also carry gun if the site require them to carry gun. The owner of the site will request for the armed guard.

Unarmed guard are those that not required to carry gun, they are to observe and detect also to report.

Uniformed security wears their uniform to work in other to be recognize as a security officer both armed and unarmed security can be a uniformed security. They must wear their uniformed while they are on duty and be neat and ready. Undercover security may not require to wear the uniform, some carry gun and some other did not require in a department store, some undercover did not carry gun they work around the store to observed the customer of what they doing and they can also arrest the wrong doing customer. Private security and private investigations deal with the government as long as they satisfy the government requirement to be a security firm. A security officer must be nice and vigilant to the people around them especially the employee of the company, let me give you a tip of security guard, suppose I walk inn to the building you are securing and I know you are hungry like a hungry-jack and drop a $20 note down near you, as a security guard; will you ask me if I drop any money down by mistake or you will keep the money, my answer to that is that it depends. A good security officer must be trusted, that is why they put him there to secure the site.

There are factors to be consider before making an arrest. At no time are you as a security guard obligated to make an arrest. You may be at the scene when a violation occurs, but you do not have to make an arrest. Your first responsibility should be prevention, after a violation has been committed your responsibility should be to observe and report. The purpose of the training is not to encourage you to make more arrests but to teach you the law concerning arrests, so you will know what you can and what you cannot do under the law. Some employers may want their security personnel to be more proactive as long as they stay within the parameters of what is lawful regarding private persons arrest. It is not wise for security guard that was not carrying weapon to wait for the intruder that carry weapon or is bigger in size than you are. Remember observe and report.

As a security guard, you are a representative of your employer, therefore, any negligence or wrongful acts committed by you may also cause your employer to be held responsible. Suits may be brought against you and your employer. If a security officer make a false arrest the person arrested may file a civil suit for damages against the security company.

A security officer is an agent of the owner of the private property and in this role, can exercise the owner's right to ask people on the owner's property what they are doing there, who they are, etc. If they refuse to answer the questions or if their answers are not satisfactory, the security guard may ask them to leave, if they do not leave, then the security guard may arrest them for trespassing, and should call local law enforcement without delay. The owner of the property has the right to establish certain rules on his property that may not be a part of the penal code. For instance, if an employee shows up for work drunk, he may be violating a company rule. The client may want the employee sent home or may intend to fire the employee. How this situation is handled is between the employer and the employee, and has nothing to do with the police or public law. A security officer must know what the employer's policy states.

A security guard trying to enforce company policy could, however resulted in a violation of public law. If the employee is asked to leave and refuses, he may be arrested for violating the public law against trespassing. On the other hand, if the security guard uses unnecessary force in removing the employee from the premises, the security officer may be arrested for committing assault or battery. As a security officer acting as a representative of the owner on the owner's private property, you can physically prevent a person from entering an area, but only as a last resort, be sure to check with your employer regarding the way handle a violation of company rules as well as how to handle violation of certain law.

The very nature of security work requires security personnel to be constantly aware of their surroundings, the law and the mission of private security in today's society. Consider the facts involved in the incident, the questions will be Who, What, When, Where, How, and Why those six questions must be able to be answer by a security officer. When any one is a private property, the owner has a right to make a law withing his properties, he can order guard to check all the employees bags and pocket before they live the compound. That will be okay as long he let the employee knows what he want the security guard to do. If the employee fail to co-operate with the security guard then the guard should record the case down and forward to the superior. The guard should describe the necessary information in the report such as date, time, and the location of the place, license plate number of the car and physical description.

Security guard cannot carry handguns and batons unless authorized by the Bureau. Security guards are allowed to carry an exposed firearm and or baton only after the security guard completes the Bureau recognized training and the appropriate permits are issued. A private person making a misdemeanor arrest may be found criminally liable for a false arrest if the arrest is made and the arresting party did not actually observe the suspect commit the misdemeanor in his presence.

When I was working as a security guard officer, and at the same time I am a student going to full time school. The reason why I take this job is because, when I come back from school I will have time for myself to relax before going back to work, and when I get to work, I have some little time to study and read my books and do my home work. I always take caution because you will never know who will come inn to disturb you. Can you blame the folk of the town what they are innocent of doing and capable of doing it. When I was on duty, the guard must make rounds, clocking the keys and also calling inn to the answering machine.

Everyday I used the elevator to take me upstairs and to the basement. I saw nothing, nobody in the building. Supposing whenever I was on the elevator, nobody ever come to stop the elevator so that they can do their business of burglarizing the building but in this case no suspicious.

Furthermore, sometimes it will be two or three security guard officers on duty at the same time on one shift, from 8.00Pm to the 8.00Am in the morning. But this time it is me only because our office thinks the area is less crime when there is no incident reported for many years and this allowed the company to retain our contract with them. But on this days, after several years, I was making my rounds, calling inn, making observations, I see nobody enter into the building, I see no door break into. In the morning I make reports that everything is secure. When I come back in the night to report for duty they will tell me that the building has been broke into during the night shift, I said what!, why, I make report that everything is secure before I left the building, but to my surprise there is nothing we can do about it. The incident was repeated again and again. Now the office send inn the security guard officer with firearms to come and work with me but it's no avail. So now it is clear that those rubbers want to burglarize the company. So I will have to leave the site to the security guard officer with firearms, and I was sent to another site.

A truly great workplace culture is composed of many different faces. From the way you hire to the coffee you serve in the restaurant, but the most important aspect is the workplace itself. In many ways what your office look like is a direct representation of your work culture. It is the physical embodiment of your beliefs, your standards and your theories on how to treat your employees and run your business, and you don't want visitors to question any of your idea.

No one can think clearly and efficiently when they are surrounded in on all side by bunch of looming files, not only is it visually unpleasant, but clutter also has a subconscious effect of adding crazy junk to their daily life. One of my best clients is a business called nurse aid, which provides home health care services. I never worked for these company before but a friend of my was, the first time I visited their office, I was shocked. There were boxes everywhere, stack of file falling, dred colors, scratched and dented furniture basically, it was not really the kind of environment people would not typically feel compelled to be productive in the shareholders weren't slobs, they were just focused on running their rapidly growing business, on my advice nurse next door endeavored to uncluttered and clean and that ridiculous has since become part of the company's business culture.

The change has been profound. The energy in the building is drastically better, employee's moods have changed and more people can fit into the space without it feeling crowded. In fact the owner's been looking into bigger offices before the clean up. However, let me be clear that I am not suggesting you spend hours each day scrubbing, the idea is to keep the office free of unnecessary clutter, broken office equipment, old files, retired computers and anything that can be stored, donated or scrapped. People should get an instant idea what your company is like the moment they walk through the door, and a dingy disorderly space sends the wrong message. How clean is your workplace, do you have clean up days.

You can do anything if you put your mind into it, failure is not an option although there is failure in every entrepreneur's future, the non quitting spirits is not giving up when your business going down, you will thank those that help you. Patience is a virtue, the lesson of patience is an essential characteristic that small business owners need to learn. Most overnight success took many years. The rapid rise to financial fortune is only a fairy tale that is primarily realized only after the exit event. By their very nature, entrepreneurs are not a patient group, but they need to take a longer term view in order to be successful. Most entrepreneurs are not successful on their first try or second.

Punctuality and getting tasks done on time are critical skills for small business, don't be late, you can not say because is your business that you can get there anytime you kike. What you do, is what your employees will also do. In order words, if you are never on time or don't complete tasks in timely manner, and your staff won't either. Stop complaining about the job you do, try and make your note interesting to your staff. In business, while you can't control the outcome, you can control your responsibility. Learn what you can from current result and move on by taking an action that gives another chance of success.

Good things come to those who wait, most small business owners get tired of just waiting, they go out there and make things happen. To be successful, value pro activity over reactivity. Do what you like doing and the money will follow; that also a guarantee. In any aspect of our lives, If we do what we love workers, businessman, and not thinking otherwise, should be a success.

There was a time, although it's hard to believe it now, before the internet a time when the landlines telephone ruled the desk, when a secretary took down messages and a pocket calculator did the math, some remember it. Back in 1980, the office was a perforated paper trail, all communication and organization was about paper, in and out, trays were our only communication between the employees, all appointment and contacts were bundle in one place, and the stationary cupboard was filled with staplers, paper clips, floppy disk, rubber stamps and hole punches. So I was not total surprise that the digital world is taking place and filling the gap that was suppose to handle by humans.

What do you think of when you think of a small business, maybe words like flexibility and innovation come to mind. But for many of the businesses profiled on the following pages, size represents a more fundamental freedom. The freedom to be themselves and the chance to take control of their own destinies. They're cool entrepreneurs corporate workers who've decided to do it alone; mother who've found new and a fulfilling ways to meld their working and personal lives and ethical entrepreneur those who've aimed to use their business as a platform to influence or effect social changes.

The innovative business models such as these are leading the way in the new economy, no one read the business journals or have five year plans, in other words they renew our plan every year and kind of made it up as we went along, or just owing a profitable business can enough to provide for your future if you make the most of it. Consider whether the accounts and the institutions behind them will make your life easier or harder. The best best business practice is to make things simpler and easy to reach when needed. We will not go too deep with business transactions and how they practices their business but just to show about what is going on in a typical security firms and it affiliates.

Finally remember too that the tax man likes to see exactly how you've spent your money. Keep business and personal account separate. Make available to all your receipts, or at least be sure your accounts provide good reporting, with quarterly and annual statement summaries.

That can do attitude may be as old as America itself, but today's entrepreneurs are finding their own ways of following their dreams. We know we had a great idea, but we were so determined to make it work, we'd have slept on the floor if we had to, we thought if we don't do it now we're never going to and whatever happens it will certainly be a great learning experience. At least we have that kind of common sense attitude to begin with.

The mixture, and the joy that at last it will fall on our side, is the basic idea, and what to do, even though you did not believe that you trespass. You were an employee of a company but the idea supporting your position could not be ratify at that time. That mixture of leap in the dark faith and dauntless enthusiasm is key to success of all the following entrepreneurs. Having said all this, eating bad food, or know money to buy more food, I know it will be at the back of your head for my brawny. They can not help you, nor support you, or get you what you really want. The society may change and economies may boom, and bust, but the spirit of adventure that drives the small business pioneer remain one of the eternal verities. No wonder corporate giants can only look on in awe on envy as the latest left-field start-up races through the field to envy the public imagination.

When you think of what makes a business healthy, you probably focus on measures like profits, sales growth or customer logicality, but you can have all of those things and still go out of business if you don't have the one thing that all companies need, such as cash. It takes cash to pay employees, to pay the rent and to keep the doors open and the lights on. Money laundry in the office or to keep the checks open that anyone can walk in and take some check and ran out the door will be a disaster to the company. The company need the employee that can be trusted and not to imbecile the company money or spend the money any how. When the expenses is much more than the profits, that means the company will probably go bankrupt.

Cash flow issues will not be obvious from even the most careful review of a company's income statement. Cash and how your company is using it, can only be seen on the balance sheet and cash flow statements. Sales, expenses and profits are important of course, but an income statement represents only a moments in time. A cash flow statement on the other hand shows the movement of money in and out of the business over a period of time.

To prevent cash shortages, the best defense is a good offense, to get serious about minimizing fixed expenses. A company should be big enough to cover only its most predictable recurring needs. Consistent growth is the best way to smooth out bumps in cash flow.

When opportunities for growth present themselves the advantage can be taken.

On this security issue, we learn that by definition, your brand is the distinctive name identifying your products. But beyond your name it's the associations that people make when they think about your business. It is a unique identifier of your business, the efficiency of your service and the memorable nature of the overall experience. Over time we have built immunity to corporate jargon, and in doing so, we have discounted the significant of branding as a useful tool in developing a successful business.

But not to worry much about what is going on around, the business will sell itself if the value is good. Of course, the principal concern for any business entrepreneur is developing the best product or service in their field, with excellent as standard a business is in an enviable position. Your brand plays a key role in differentiating you from the competition and helps communicate your key message to the consumer, I think enough say about the security firm and the carpet firm that work hand to hand and support each other, despite there are nothing there except the contract.

In a typical firm, the racial tension can be the focus point, but for the employee of the firm must focus and not to pay too much attention to the issue that can make him a mistake or cause an embarrassment to your work. The old adage the rules were made to be broken simply doesn't apply to branding, you may add or update, but the rules is you create for your own brand should stand the test of time. No argument made here about your decisions once you have decided the brand, there should be one thing imprinted on your consciousness, and even on your subconscious and that's the very thing that sets your product or service apart from every other in the market, no one say this is a true statement on how you want your business to be run but you get the idea, do your business and do it firm.

Times have changed. Long gone are the days when all you needed to do to reach the biggest audience was buy advertising. Agencies now offer other new way to explore, in addition to advertising in print and on TV, sometimes the most effective means of reaching your audience are far from traditional way. The channels by which we communicates are forever changing and multiplying, the internet in particular has revolutionized the way we communicate, not only between each other, but with our favorite companies. Word of mouth has always been the most powerful tools for advertising. While it can be difficult to quantify, it is a very effective medium, in many cases it's free and it's a very attractive marketing method.

Sustainability makes sense for the environment and for business. For the small business owner with tight margins, there are a multitude of benefits to adopting a more sustainable approach.

For a new start or for a business that established its reputation and stream line nature by spending less on resources and creating instant savings will be the opposite of expensive investments. I hope we touch some aspect of the security firm and the big company behind them that support them and award them their contract. Also, hope that their administrations, the rules to follow provide us an insight.

CHAPTER FOUR

Computer

The earliest known tool for use in computation was the abacus, and it was thought to have been invented in Babylon circa 2400 BC. Its original style of usage was by lines drawn in sand with pebbles to count. Abacus of a more modern design, are still used as calculation tools today. This was the first known computer and most advanced system of calculation known to date. The word for calculus means "Pebble or stone" and is the name given to a branch of mathematics. A person well skilled in the use of the abacus often can match the speed of a hand held electronic calculator for simple operations such as addition and subtraction.

Mechanical analog computer devices appeared again a thousand years later in the medieval Islamic world and were developed by Muslim astronomers. Long before mechanical calculating devices were invented, astronomers, navigators, and scientists relied on books of tables for their calculations. These were completed by hand, typeset, and printed. Needless to say calculations carried out by humans were subject to human errors and the transcribing and typesetting, produced additional errors. Thus, a new system had to be devised. The seventeenth century mathematician Blaise Pascal and Gottfried Wilhelm Leibniz attacked this problem by developing mechanical calculators that could perform the basic mathematical function of addition, subtraction, multiplication, and division and could do so with speed and fairly good accuracy. However, there were still problems with the creation and use of these devices, such as difficulties in building them. While some improvements were made from these early designs, in truth, computing machinery didn't show much improvement for almost 200 years. The history of computing is longer than the history of computing hardware and modern computing technology and includes the history of methods intended for pen and paper or chalk and slate, with or without the aid of tables.

Computing is intimately tied to the representation of numbers. But long before abstractions like the number arose, there were mathematical concepts to serve the purposes of civilization. These concepts are implicit in a solid practices. Eventually, the concept of numbers became a solid and familiar enough for counting to arise, at times with sing-song mnemonics to teach sequences to others. Advances in the numerical system and mathematical notation eventually led to the discovery of mathematical operations such as addition, subtraction, multiplication, division, squaring, square root, and so forth. The operations were formalized, and concepts about the operations because understood well enough to be stated formally, and even proven, but none of the early computational devices were really computers in the modern sense, and it took considerable advancement in mathematics and theory before the first modern computers could be designed.

By the Middle Ages, the positional Hindu-Arabic numeral system had reached Europe, which allowed for systematic computation of numbers. During this period, the representation of a calculation on paper actually allowed calculation of mathematical expression, and the tabulation of mathematical functions such as the square root and the common logarithm for use in multiplication and division and the trigonometric functions. Englishman Charles Babbage authored a scientific paper in 1822 called "On the Theoretical principles of the machinery for Calculating Tables", which included a proposal to construct a machine called the Difference Engine designed to mechanize the production of tables. Later, Babbage changed his concept to an Analytical Engine that would be programmable. Babbage ideas were well received by the Royal astronomical Society, but circumstances prevented him from completing his project before his death in 1871. Though Babbage did not live to see it happen, he had a profound effect on computer technology, His use of punched cards as a storage device was 100 years ahead of its time, and the concepts of separate storage and computation units persist to these very day.

During the United State census of 1890, basic computing concepts evolved significantly. When the census had be done in 1880, it took eight years to process and tabulate the data. To speed up this precess, Herman Hollerith built an electromechanical unit that processed information on punched cards. The inventor used the punched card to record information such as age, sex, nationality, and other vital statistics. While punched cards are no longer used in connection with computers,parts of Hollerith's code are still used to instruct computers on how to read input and format output.

In the 1940s, the first fully electronic calculator to compute complex equations was constructed by j. Presper Eckert and John W. Mauchly. The unit did speed up the solving of complex mathematical problems but could not be programmed in the sense that we use that term today. Instead, it had to be rewired by hand to solve new problems. And when one of its almost 18,000 vacuum tubes failed which happened quite often, the system could not work properly.

The 1948 development of the transistor by Bell Telephone Laboratories helped overcome this problem. With transistors, it was now possible to hand-wire basic operations into the computer itself, doing away with bulky and temperamental vacuum tubes and replacing them with smaller, more work were able to get done.

Mathematician scientist John Von Neumann made another important contribution with his concept of store programs. This revolutionized the ease and speed with which a computer could be programmed, Von Neumann has been credited with defining the basic structure or design of the modern electronic digital computer. Without the development of the semiconductor integrated circuit, however, the industry would undoubtedly have been confined to expensive specialized machines with only limited use.

During the next couple of decades, the creation of increasingly powerful mainframe computers dominated the art and science of computing. But then in the 1970s and 1980s, a revolution occurred. The development and popularization of microcomputers eventually known as personal computers brought computing into homes, small businesses, offices, and virtually every type of organization. Then a dizzying array of developments made computing increasingly important for science, technology, commerce,and everyday personal life. The miniaturization of computer chips and other components, the creation of the Internet, the growth of Email and the development of increasingly fast and powerful computers are just a few of these advancements.

In year twenty-five century, computers are no longer new on the scene. To the contrary, computer are everywhere. They are valued by society and, as a result, so are the computer scientists, systems analysts, software developers, and other specialists who work with them. For those who have elected to pursue training in computer science, information technology, or related areas, the future appears bright indeed.

Computer and peripheral equipment operators oversee the operation of computer hardware systems, ensuring that these machines are used as efficiently as possible. This means that operators must be proactive anticipate problems before they occur and take preventive action, as well as solve problems that do occur. Duties of computer and peripheral equipment operators vary with the policies of the employer, the size of the installation, and the kind of equipment used. Working from operating instruction prepared by programmers, users, or operations managers, computer operators set controls on the computer and on peripheral devices required to run a particular job. Computer operators on peripheral devices required to run a particular job. Computer operators or, in some large installation, peripheral equipment operators had the equipment with tapes, disks, and paper as needed. While the computer is running which may be twenty-four hours a day for large computers, computer operators monitor the computer console and respond to operating and computer message occurs. Operators must locate and solve the problem or terminate the program.

Traditionally, peripheral equipment operators have to prepare printout and other output for distribution to computer users. Operators also maintain log books listing each job that is run and events such as machine malfunctions that occurred during their shift. In addition, computer operators may supervise and train peripheral equipment operators and computer operator trainees. They also may help programmers and systems analysis test and debug new program.

As the trend toward networking computers accelerates, a growing number of these workers are operating PCs and minicomputers. More and more establishments are recognizing the need to connect all their computer to enhance productivity. In many offices, factories, and other work settings, PCs and minicomputers serve as the center of such networks, often referred to as local area (LAN) or many users systems. Although some of these computers are operated by users in the area, many require the services of full time operators. The tasks performed are very similar to those performed on the larger computers.

As technology evolves, machines become more impressive, dwarfing humans in their capabilities but ultimately needing the human. A big machine use for cleanup is formidable compared with the trail biological creature who drives it. The big machine can be highly automated, but it needs a driver. Bond traders have worldwide networks of computers that can detect and take advantage of fleeting investment opportunities. A jumbo jet pilot has little to do as more and more functions are performed more reliably by computers than by the pilot. But jumbo jets are not likely to fly without human pilots. By contrast, the flight attendant's job has little automation. The more the basic mechanisms become automated, the greater the need for people to concentrate on uniquely human roles such as inventing new ways to delight the customers.

Much of a corporation's expertise and procedures are represented on its software. Corporate software is rapidly growing in complexity, encapsulating an ever-growing body of human know how. Software that can be purchased is growing more comprehensive and sophisticated. Designers of corporate operations need to ask what should be done by software, The machine can performed very well, depend on how the human counterpart thinks and build the machine. The compiler execute a series of instruction in which programer wrote and tell the programer if the instruction is okay. There many compiler today that answer the question the programer ask from his program.

Computer programmers write and maintain the detailed instructions, called programs or software, that list in a logical order the steps that computer must take to execute, and to perform their functions.

In many large organizations, programmers follow descriptions prepared by systems analysts who have carefully studied the task that the computer system is going to perform. These descriptions list the input required, the steps the computer must follow to process data, and the desired arrangement of the output. Some organizations, particularly smaller ones, do not employ systems analysts. Instead, workers called programmer-analysts are responsible for both systems analysis and programming. Regardless of setting of corporation the programmers write specific programs by breaking down each step into a logical series of instructions the computer can follow. They then code these instructions in a high level programming language.

The growing use of packaged software, such as spreadsheet and database management software packages, allow users to write simple programs to access data and perform calculations. Programmers in software development companies may work directly with experts from various fields to create software, either programs designed for specific clients or packaged software general use, ranging from games and educational software to programs for desktop publishing, financial planning, and spreadsheets. Much of the programming been done today is in the area of packaged software development, one of the most rapidly growing segments of the computer industry.

Programmers often are grouped into two broad types, Application programmers and Systems programmers. Applications programmer usually are oriented toward business, engineering, or science. They write software designed to handle specific jobs, such as a program used to do an inventory control system, they also may work to revise the existing package software. Systems programmers on the other hand, maintain the software that controls the operation of an entire computer system, These workers make changes in the sets of instructions that determine how the central processing unit of the system handles the various jobs it been given and communicates with peripheral equipment, such as terminals, printers, and disk drives.

Today computers get sense, diversity of automatic sensors are used. Bar codes at Supermarket checkout at the counters can provide immediate information about sales to the computer system that plan purchase, restocking, distribution, pricing, and advertising. Containers shipped around the world can have transponders so that their whereabouts are known. Satellite transmitters on trucks are inexpensive. Global positioning satellite (GPS) electronics enable computers to aware of the position of cars, trucks, containers, and so forth, accurate to 100 feet or less. Computers can track the location of people who use portable phone.

In 1994 the internet took a great step forward because the World Wide Web (WWW) came into general use. The Web allows users to mouse-click on highlighted words or icons to select new pages or files of information. The data selected in this way can be anywhere on the Net. You can click on any Web page that provide you with menu and you can browse any web pages in the internet.

In 1996 another innovation represented a quantum leap in Web capability was also brought to life, the downloading of not just messages and data from the net but also chunks of program that could be executed in one's computer. The program chunks called applets, little applications are written in a language called Java. All different types of computers can have an interpreter that enables them to run java applets. The information obtained from the Net can then be brought to life. There can be animated Web pages, cartoon like, helpers, applications for placing orders or calculating expense reports, details of a products, option packaged with programs to compute its total cost, and all the diversity that programming can bring.

In many organizations computer security measure are feeble, and this weakness invites misuse. A corporate network should be designed to have tight security and should not be connected to the Internet without protection. There should be airlocks between public networks and private internal networks. The tern firewall describes a small computer through which traffic has to pass to travel from and insecure network to a secure network. It may be used to authenticate messages from the Internet before passing them to corporate intranet.

Messages are taken into a filter and subjected to various tests before they are put on the internal corporate network. Some systems automatically translate internal network addresses, so that the internal systems are shielded, and allow only certain types of packets to reach certain machines. Sometimes multiple firewalls are used within organizations to isolate separate security domains. The software and hardware facilities designed to provide protection are constantly being improved.

A web server can make a vast amount of information available, it often lists topics such as product catalog, announcements, optional features, price lists, help with problems, frequently asked questions user comments, suggestions, and so forth. Users who contact the Web site can select a topic, explore its contents, and post messages. They can also download files or exchange information with other users. They may post a question that a specialists may need to answer. The site may contain operating manuals, maintenance manuals, troubleshooting guidelines, software, photographs, lectures, or presentation. Changes can be posted constantly and are thus immediately available to all users. This is far faster and cheaper than distributing amendments to large paper documents. Web server allow more question and answer and let customer interact with one another.

The term virtual means that something appears to exist and is used as though it exists when in actuality it does not. A computer may have a virtual memory of 256 megabytes when its real memory is 16 megabytes, the computer appears to have a larger memory because it quickly transfers memory contents from its disks when needed, like a computer producing more memory. A virtual circuit appears to exist and is used as though it exists, but in reality it is derived by transmitting packets through a network.

In 1854, English mathematician George Boole published his system of Boolean algebra, which stated that everything in the universe could be represented using the numbers 0 and 1. He thought of the numbers 0 and 1 as nothing and universe. Though the concept of either existing or not existing may seem obvious to us now, this was a revolutionary new advance in thinking about numbers. In fact the 0 and 1 have exist by the man called Leibniz the mathematician and inventor that he never complete his work before his death.

A binary number system is a system in which numbers and letters are represented by only two digits, 0 and 1. Our commonly used decimal number system uses the 10 digits 0 through 9. The binary number system is well suited to computers because an electrical switch that is OFF can represent zero and an electrical switch that is ON can represent 1.

American standard Code for Information Interchange (ASC11-8), represents the letters of the alphabet using only two symbols, 0 [zero] and 1, ASC11-8 is a code that was developed to enable higher-level computer languages to be represented by combinations of the binary numbers 0 and 1 in groups of eight. Each 0 and 1 in the binary numbers system is called a bit and a group of eight bits is known as a byte. When talking about computers, a word is a group of bits, usually 8 to 64 bits or more in size. For example.

Character	ASC11-8
a	11100001
b	11100010
c	11100011 and so on to z
z	11111010

And for the number to binary code, computer can not calculate using 1,2,3,4 as the human calculate, the computer use the binary code to calculate and translate to human digital number. For example, to convert the the decimal to binary assume the number is 128. The binary use base 2 to calculate it goes like this

128	64	32	16	8	4	2	1
1	0	0	0	0	0	0	0

You can see when you calculate by yourself at the rate of base 2 you will arrive at 128 decimal. Here are some sample of binary number to decimal and to hexadecimal.

Hexadecimal	Binary	Decimal
0	0000	0
1	0001	1
2	0010	2
3	0011	3
4	0100	4
5	0101	5
6	0110	6
7	0111	7
8	1000	8
9	1001	9
A	1010	10
B	1011	11
C	1100	12
D	1101	13
E	1110	14
F	111	15
10	00010000	16

Also consider this binary for practice by converting the binary to decimal and hexadecimal.

000
001
010
011
100
101
110
111

The base representation.

Representation	Base
EFFE11	base-16 hexadecimal
15728145	base-10 decimal
1101111110001	base-2 binary.

Among the instructions computer uses to perform its operations are Boolean Operators. Boolean operators define the relationships between words or groups of words. Another operators that you can use for computer operations.

Boolean Operators
AND
OR
NOT

Since computers operate in binary (using zero and ones), Computer logic can often expressed in Boolean terms. For example, a true statement returns a value of 1, while a false statement return a value of 0. of cause, most calculations require more than a simple true/false statement. Therefore, computer processors perform complex calculations by linking multiple binary (or Boolean) statements together. Complex Boolean expressions can be expressed as a series of logic gate.

CPU stands for "Central Processing Unit" It's pretty much the brain of a computer. It processes everything from basic function for complex programs. Anything that needs to be computed, it is sent to the CPU. In terms of computing power, the CPU is the most important element of a computer. Often in powerful computers such a dedicated servers there a 2 or more CPU used. There are four steps that nearly all CPU use in their operation and there are fetch, decode, execute and output. The first step fetch the task, involves retrieving an instruction from program memory. In the decode steps, the instruction is broken up into parts that have significance to other portions of the CPU, such as the arithmetic logic unit (ALU). The final steps is write back the output, simply write back the result.

The operating program, or system, oversees or manages the workings of the computer itself. The operating system is adapted to enhance the characteristics or architecture of a particular type of computer. For example, most IBM compatible personal computers use Microsoft MS-DOS as their operating system. In addition to operation systems there are applications programs that instruct the computer to do specific tasks.

In the Memory section, is a place to store data and instructions. Data and instructions needed for calculations or problem solving are stored in a computer's memory. If a computer has more than one processor, each processor may have it own memory and may in addition share a central memory with the other processors. A computer has a place to store information that is needed for immediate use as well as a place to store more permanent information that may be needed in the future.

The final task in the CPU is the input and output of information. Because of the high volume of data and their high speeds of operation, its need another computers to oversee the input and output of information. Input is the data fetch inn or information that a user enters into the computer through the key-board to solve a calculation or problem. After the calculation and the problem solve, the user may need to get the result out by means of console, printer, and other devises. I think you get some idea about how the computer was made how it operate. The scientist uses computer in many various field. I will mention some part of it as we continue. Now you purchase your computer and you bring it home, you will need to hook it up and connect the rest of the component to the system unit such as printer, external storage devises, monitor, key-board and speakers.

After everything is properly positioned, you can now connect the computer to the electrical outlet,

1. press the button on the monitor or flip its switch to turn it on. Computer manufacturers recommend that you turn on the monitor fist. This allows you to see the start-up messages, and it prevents the monitor's power surge from passing through the system unit's components. On many newer computers, the monitor turns on automatically when you turn on the system unit. In other case, this is not true with desktop computers, only laptops and net books can operate that way.

Turn on the printer if it has a power button or switch. Be sure the online light is lit not blinking. If the light is blinking, be sure the printer has paper and then press the online or power button if the printer has an online button. If you have speakers or other devices connected to your computer, then turn them on. Press the power button or flip the switch on the system unit.

What happens next varies from on computer to another. Most computers perform a series of start-up tests, load a set of instructions, and display text messages on the monitor. These messages typically disappear before you have time to read them. Your computer then runs its operating system, windows. On most computer PCs, although some PCS run Linux and Macintosh computers run Mac OS. The operating system provides the instructions your computer needs to function.

Windows prompts you to log on by clicking your user name, if a log—on screen does not appear, your computer is set up for a single user and does not require a password to log on. If a log-on screen does appear, click your user name and then if requested, enter the password that has been assigned to this user account. At this point, you're ready to start working on your computer. If the windows desktop is displayed as it should, you can click the Start button in the lower-left corner and point to ALL PROGRAMS to check out which games and programs are installed on your computer.

Your computer is not a refrigerator, if you power it down properly, nothing you have stored in it is going to lost but if you do not properly shot it down, and you did not save your work, every thing will get lost. You're not going to wear out the power button by turning your computer off at the end of your weekday and turning it on the next morning. Nor are you going to harm the electrical components inside the computer by turning it off and on. In fact, keeping your computer running when it's not in use subjects the components to more heat which can lessen their useful lives. You can significantly reduce the amount of energy your computer uses by taking these steps turn it off when you're not using it, and make the most of your computer's built in power saving features.

When you start a PC-personal computer, (a compatible computer), it automatically runs some version of the operating system called windows. There are many types of window in the market today, ranging from window XP, vista,98 and much more. It even comes complete with it own desktop utilities, including a calculator, a notepad, and so on. You can now go ahead by checking out the windows desktop. When you first start your computer, your new desktop appears very neat. Several icons (small pictures) dot the surface of the Windows desktop and a strip called task bar appears at the bottom of the screen. The start button opens a menu containing the names of all the programs installed on your computer.

This chapter is to give you a glimpse knowledge about computer, by now it pretty clear that you have a little idea about how your computer is all about. How it started and what it can do. Finally with your computer, a modem, and a subscription to an Internet service provider, you can do much more by ordering online, send email, send your resume to prospect employer's, just practically every thing we can do in our real time. The Internet computers are all interconnected by a massive collection of fiber-optic cables, phone lines, and wireless signals that enable the Internet to transfer data at lightning-fast speeds. The network of cables, phone lines, and wire-less connections that carry the data are known as the Internets backbone

Now we are all reliance on gadgets, and on instant high speed access to the internet. Many people use internet as their sole medium of business transactions. It has been a similar story for many other workplace tools. For many years, the way we work has changed faster than most of us can believe.

As the speed and reliability of our accessories such as cell phone, digital organizer, internet fast speed modem connections improved so did the usefulness of the internet. It because and integral part of work life multiplying productivity and facilitating the way business is run. E-commerce change the world of work beyond recognition, combined with the laptop, the desk top also have a lesser impact.

To be connected to the Internet, your computer need modem. Most today's computer came with installed modem, but the old computer; some of them do not have modem, but the new computer technology majority of them come with modem. After you check your modem and is working alright then you can go ahead and apply for the ISP of your choice. Also some computer came with free ISP subscription for certain time, then you can enroll in any of them. After the enrollment is completed you are now ready to launch your computer to the internet. Good luck.

If you live in a major metropolitan area, you have plenty of internet connection to choose from, dial-up using a standard modem over your existing phone line, DSL modem, cable modem, satellite and perhaps even some type of wireless connection mobile. Consider this factors before making decision are availability, You might not have cable or DSL service in your area, so that can significantly limit your choices, Dial-up service over an existing phone line and satellite service are almost universally available. The second choice is speed, you should choose the fastest connection you can afford, you may think you won't use the Internet that much faster, but when windows or your other programs need to download huge software updates, you will be wishing you had a faster connection. The last one is price, monthly service charges range from about $5.99 per month for dial-up services plus the cost of local phone service, so the cost maybe high for some people.

The internet is a good place to be, just play with photos and play games or download what ever you wants. The actual store can not be replace. It doesn't matter whether you're large or small business, a supermarket with 100 branches or an organic grocer with one you have the same chance to succeed!. If you can spread the word effectively you have the opportunity to advertise your services to an international audience and generate their interest. Create reasons for your customers to keep returning to your website, Updated news, blogs, pod casts or special offers are just some of the many ways to attract customer.

The networks works like, as you are connecting to the internet. There are two basic types of networks; are client server and peer-to-peer networks. On a client server network, all computers are wired to a central computer. When ever you need to access a network resources, you connect to the server which process your commands and requests, links you connect to the other computers, and provides access to shared equipment and other resources. Although some what expensive, and difficult to set up, a client server network offers two big advantages over the peer-to-peer networks. The client server networks allow easy to maintain centrally through the network server, and it ensures reliable data transfer. Client server networks typically have a network administration who is in charge of assigning access privilege to each computer on the network. The administrator assigns each user a user name and password. You then must enter your user name and password to log on to the networks.

On the other side of the coins, Peer-to-peer network computers are linked directly to each other without the use of a central computer. Each computer has a network card connected through a network cable to another computer or to a central hub (a connection box). Many home users and small business use this peer-to-peer configuration because it doesn't require and expensive network server and it's relatively easy to set up. However, a peer-to-peer network does have a few drawbacks, it is more difficult to manage, more vulnerable to packet collision and not very secure because no central computer is in charge of validating user identities.

For Ethernet, you need an Ethernet hub with enough ports to connect all the computers on the network. Each computer must have an Ethernet card often called an NIC or network interface card, and you need enough Ethernet cable to connect each computer to the hub. To connect computers in a wireless network (Wi-Fi) network, each computer must be equipped with a compatible wireless networking adapter. If you plan to share a high-speed Internet connection, the modem that establishes and maintains the connection to the Internet must be connected to the router so the computers that also connect to the router can share the Internet connection. The router controls the data flow between the internet and your networked computers and it secures the network from unauthorized user.

Another kind of computer you should familiarize yourself with is laptop and net-book. Both computer are similar in nature such as size and the operating system. The advantages of laptop is that you can carry it to anywhere to use, to do your home work and for personal business. Laptop is ideal for a business man that use computer to do his business, and store the information that he will need at instant.

A net-book also called a mini-laptop, sub-notebook, or mobile internet devices, both laptop and mini-laptop has these key features. Compact size and light weight, notebook are lighter than laptop, usually below around 3 pounds, and come in a smaller size than a conventional laptop. The smaller size is achieved with a smaller screen typically 10 inches or less and a smaller keyboard that doesn't have full size keys.

Net-book processor have a number of different processors. You can not compare or expect the performance you get from a conventional laptop with a faster CPU. Notebooks aren't designed to be high performance computers, however, this isn't to say they're as slow as low CPU. Instead of horsepower, the processor focus on the processor that provides decent performance with low power consumption.

The net-books storage models come with a variety of internal storage options. Solid state drives (SSD) are the wave of the future and use memory chips to store data. They're lighter and have no moving parts to malfunction, but they're currently more expensive and hold a limited amount of data compared with traditional hard drives. Hard drives add a bit more weight to a notebook, and offer more storage space at a lesser price than an SSD.

The net-book keyboard size is small in a way to fit a notebook in such a small package, manufactures need to make some compromises, and one of them is the size of the keyboard. Different models have different reduced size keyboards. Some users with larger hands and fingers may find it difficult to type on a smaller keyboards, the size if tge jets cab vary between manufacturers and models. Most 10 inches screen net-books have very usable keyboards although they are reduced in size.

Because of the notebook small size and portable nature, net-books get a lot of use while on the road or around the house, either for business or pleasure, net-book especially useful for the following reasons. (a) checking and sending e-mail, (b) browsing the web, © watching videos, (d) listening to music, (e) instant messaging and using Skype, (f) working on word processing and spreadsheet documents when away from a primary computer(desk top), (g)viewing digital photos, (h) traveling on airplanes, trains, and buses. If your net-book uses Microsoft Windows as its operating system, then its compatible with all windows programs with the exception of some games and other graphic are limited because of the net-book memory resources.

If you decide you need more memory, the next question you must ask yourself is whether your net-book's RAM can be upgraded. Turn to your user manual for the answer or the manufacture's support web site. If you're set on upgrading memory, I certainly won't discourage you. Memory is relatively cheap and depending on the net-book model, it is pretty easy to install. In fact these factors don't absolutely mean you can't upgrade the memory, they just make it more difficult and mean there are more potential consequences if you mess up, however if you're technically inclined and if it's possible to upgrade the memory and if you don't care about the warranty then carry on. If you stuck with a net-book that you can't upgrade, don't worry, just try and make a best of it.

I hope we all have an idea about what computer is, and what it can do. A device designed to help us manage and enjoy our lives more fully. You can use a computer to type and print a letter, also the latest computer technology can completely revolutionize your professional and as well as personal life.

CHAPTER FIVE

Health

I am not a medical writers, I read it and study it myself, but we need to touch some points on the subject because of the experience, If you have been following this text book you will realize that your health is very important because the healthful life come first, then everything follow it. Your sexual habits, your life style, weather changes, cold, hot, and much more.

Medical writers upon this subject are comparatively numerous in French and German literature, and they have been multiplying rapidly of late years. The phenomenon of sexual inversion is usually regarded in this books from the point of view of psychopathic or neuropathic derangement, inherited from morbid ancestors, and developed in the patient by early habits of self-abuse.

What is the exact distinction between "psychopathic" and "peripheral neuropathy" I do not know. The former term seems intelligible in the theologian's theory. But I cannot understand both being used together to indicate different kinds of pathological diathesis. What is the soul, what are the nerves? We have probably to take the two terms as indicating two ways of considering the same phenomenon; the one subjective, the other objective; "psychopathic" pointing to the personality disorder as observed in the mind emotions of its subject; "peripheral neuropathy" to the damage as observed in peripheral of the nervous system.

It would be impossible, in an essay of this kind, to review the whole mass of medical observation, inference and speculation which we have at our command. Perhaps well qualified for the task of criticism and comparison in a matter of delicacy where doctors differ as to details. They take very nearly similar views of the phenomenon; and between them they are gradually forming a theory which is likely to become widely accepted.

You see it everyday on television shows the dramatic scenes where skilled surgeons save lives right on the operating table. Surgical technologists are key members of the healthcare field, working in teams to assist with life saving procedures. They set up surgical instruments, equipment, medication and supplies before surgery. During surgery they pass these instruments and supplies to surgeons and assist by holding re tractors, cutting sutures and helping apply dressings. They learn a wide variety of key procedures used in the operating room and how to work under high pressure situations. As the population increases, there is a greater demand for medical personnel to perform same day surgical procedures. As a result, employment opportunities in surgical technology are expected to grow much faster than average. I learned much in life about medical procedures to the extend that I started to develop the disease call anemic. Anemic is a very bad disease that there is know specific cure until my doctor sturdy the disease and apply the correct medicine. I undergo several test for many years and that time I was spending money for the doctors, if not the government that support the payment it could have been a different story.

I wonder how the blood could be passing out through my body and completely lose all the blood in my body, through the nose, mouth, my rectum and from anywhere in my body. I said to myself this is impossible, I argue with my doctor that you should know what is causing the blood to be dry every time you treat me back and give me some blood, but the point is that I cannot keep living like that by relying on the blood to recuperate me back. The reason why I was not afraid is that I went to different hospital for this disease the doctor to me are the same thing.

The emergency room in some way will not know what situations will arise or what resources will be needed. It has a variety of resources available to it, human, technical, and institutional resources, some of which it owns but many of which it does not. The hospital ER needs access to medical specialists from elsewhere. It may need specialized equipment, or access to data located anywhere in the world. General hospital facilities may be brought into use that are not part of the emergency room. The staff of the emergency room responds to unexpected situations with a great sense of urgency and rapidly assembles whatever teams or resources are needed, many of them coming from other organizations. It sometimes has to use resources from direct competitors. When something happen the unexpected situations, the ambulances race out; in medical emergencies, people from different organizations expect to work together intensively, Joining their different expertise to achieve a common goal. Personnel are given the authority to command resources and to re-prioritize the allocation of these resources as situations demand. The structure of the emergency room is deliberately designed to deal with the unpredictable situations.

In the 1990s the environment of the pharmaceutical industry changed as public concern grew about the escalating cost of health care. The United States focused on managed healthcare systems that link doctors, hospitals, cost controls, and health insurance. Some of the drug companies set out to examine the overall health care problems of society to see what new roles they might play,as to they might be able to empower the public to take charge of more of certain health care problems themselves, with appropriate education, medical equipment, and access to doctors when necessary. There are various ways in which pharmaceutical companies could take a leadership role in a broader health care ecosystem.

Traditional corporations have ignored human emotion. They have tried to pretend it doesn't exist or worse, have tried to suppress it. While the chief executive was having violent temper, the middle managers were supposed to be emotionless. However, work is an emotional experience. Pride, ambition, anger, jealousy, hate, determination, fear, rage, excitement, and the kicks of accomplishment can see in employees, especially when they have their feet on the car accelerator. Negative emotions make employees tune out or actively do harm. Good emotions make employees go all out to succeed. It is a joy to do excellent work, build something special, and be recognized for it. Employees work late because they are excited about accomplishing their goals. Bad emotions have a bad effect on profit; good emotions are a fuel that drives productivity, quality, and customer satisfaction.

First of all, since this inquiry has been limited to the actual conditions of contemporary life, we need not to discuss much about the various ways in which the phenomenon of sexual inversion has been practically treated by races. After all this is a contemporary life with whose habits and religious we have no affinity. On the other hand, it is of the highest importance to obtain a correct conception of the steps whereby the christian and other religion separating themselves from ancient paganism. Introduced a new and stringent morality in their opinion on this mater and enforced their ethical views by legal prohibitions of a very formidable kind. Without prejudging, this new morality now almost universally regarded as a great advance upon the ethics of the earlier pagan world. We must observe that it arose when science was non existent, when the study of humanity had not yet emerged from the start and when theology was in the new, we have therefore to expect from it, and since no distinctions and not prejudicing, I ask are you thinking what I'm thinking, that is the question at that time. Immorality at wost should henceforth be classed as a crime against God.

Anemia is a condition in which you don't have enough healthy blood cells to carry adequate oxygen to your tissues. Having anemia may make you feel exhausted. There are many forms of anemia, each with its own cause. Anemia can be temporary or long term and it can be range from mild to sever. In the olden days of Nigeria the traditional medicine man use cocoanut shell and fire to sock the bad blood out from the patient so that the new blood can run through where the bad blood was stock in the body, but I wonder how they manage to do that and cure the patient. The blood run through the vains but how they use the tools to get the bad blood out remain mystery to me, also these type of delicate procedure can not be done in any part of the body.

In my own experiences, injury can cause blood loss through bleeding. A healthy adult can lose almost 20% of blood volume before the first symptom, restlessness, begins and 40% of volume before shock sets in. Thromboses are important for blood coagulation and the formation of blood clots, which can stop bleeding. Trauma to the internal organs or bones can cause internal bleeding, which can sometimes be severe. In my own case, I do experience all the bleeding's and internal bleeding. Dehydration can reduce the blood volume by reducing the water content of the blood. This would rarely result in shock, apart from the very severe cases but may result in hypertension and fainting.

The poor circulation of blood can be ineffective perfusion of tissues, and can be caused by a variety of conditions including blood loss, infection, poor cardiac output. When the flow of blood reduces its progression can be compounded by many causes including smoking, high blood pressure, excess circulation. Mind you this book is not for medical student or explaining medical term, it is a simple life experiences.

Anemia insufficient red cell mass, anemia can be the result of bleeding, blood disorders like nutritional deficiencies, and may require blood transfusion. Several countries have blood banks to fill the demand for transfuse blood. A person receiving a blood transfusion must have a blood type compatible with that of the donor.

The insufficient platelets can also result in bleeding disorders. Anemia a terrible disease that size both hands and the legs, not able to work or performed a functions. Just sit down in a place all day long until more blood is vessel into the body. The blood suppose to regenerate itself back if proper caution was taken place.

Substances other than oxygen can bind to hemoglobin, in some cases this can cause irreversible damage to the body. Carbon monoxide is extremely dangerous when carried to the blood via the lungs by inhalation, because carbon monoxide irreversibly binds to hemoglobin to form carbohydrate, so that less hemoglobin is free to bind oxygen, and fewer oxygen molecules can be transported throughout the blood. This can cause suffocation insidiously. A fire burning in an enclosed room with poor ventilation presents a very dangerous hazards, since it can create a build-up of carbon monoxide in the air. Some carbon monoxide binds to hemoglobin when smoking tobacco.

Leukemia is a group of cancers of the blood forming tissues. Blood is an important vector of infection. HIV, the virus that causes AIDS, is transmitted through contact with blood. Hepatitis B and C are transmitted primarily through blood contact, and also blood bone infections. Bacterial infection of the blood is bacterium. Malaria and transformations are blood borne parasitic infections.

The medical treatment for anemia range from different type of ways, such as liquid medicine, blood transfusion, and also blood rituals. Blood for transfusion is obtained from human donors by blood donation groups and stored in a blood bank till is ready to be use. There are many different blood types in humans, transfusion of blood of an incompatible blood may cause severe often fatal complication, so cross-matching is done to ensure that a compatible blood product is transfused.

Due to its importance to life, blood is associated with a large number of beliefs. One of the most basic is the use of blood as a symbol for family relationships through birth. To be related by blood is to be related by ancestry or descendant, rather than marriage. This bears closely to blood related, and sayings such as blood is thicker than water. In many religion blood is regarded as a secret source, and said the life of a creature is in the blood.

Various religious and other groups have been falsely accused of using human blood in rituals. Vampires are mythical creatures that drink blood directly for sustenance. In the vampire movies, they have all kind of unforeseen behavior that make people to scare of them. There are also other animal that drink the human blood such as leeches, Mosquitoes and others. Bats and other natural creatures so consume the blood of other animals. Blood residue can also help forensic investigations identify weapons, reconstruct a criminal action, and link suspects to the crime. Through bloodstain pattern analysis. In forensic investigation television show, it shows that forensic information can also be gained from the spatial distribution of bloodstains.

Knowledge is power, the modern executive will say knowledge is money, why knowledge creates money in many ways. The knowledge translate into market and the market translate into the money. Who does not know that money is, except people that do not aware of money. My friend, when you have money insult it, then you can have more. Knowledge constantly renewed and enhanced, is the primary source of competitive advantages. The more we enhance the products the better for market and more money will come inn. Even if there is no knowledge but you good at it, and have an idea, the more you practice the more you better off and so that is the money. Money is everything in some people mined, they can do anything to get money, and while some people says money is not everything. They probably right in the sense that is not good to be rich and loose your soul, your consent is my, so when you have money and the other does not, how do you explain that. On the side of issue, if you don't have money it will seems that the person is dead because you will need to buy something and when there is no money the feeling will not be pleasant. So love is important in man's life, love will stay for ever, money is unstable, but it must have. There are numerous book that available that deal with the aspect of our life and well being of our life, there are many ways things can go wrong through our health and well being, such as sexuality, sickness, injuries, you name it.

The other important issues about your health we can not ignore is sexual-violent or just having a fun. The young and the innocent people cannot ignore the sexuality when encounter with it. Both young woman and young man will have to dealt with their private issue, no matter how provocative it might sound.
The earlier book with some authors deals with the external aspects of inverted sexuality, as this exists in many parts of the world under the special form of prostitution. The author professes to know nothing more about the subject than what came beneath his notice in the daily practice of their duty as a informer. They writes with excusable animosity. We see at once that they are neither a philosopher by nature, nor a man of science, but only a citizen endowed with the normal citizen's antipathy for passions alien to his own. place at the head of the family of Morals, the topics was brought into collision with a tribe of people whom he

could not legally arrest, but whom he cordially hated. They were patently vicious; and what was peculiarly obvious to the normal man these degraded beings were all males. He saw that the public intolerance of anti physical passions,which he warmly shared, encouraged an organized system of chant age.

Without entertaining the question whether public opinion might be modified, he denounced the noxious gang as pests of society. The fact that country, with her legal prohibitions, suffered to the same extent as other country from the curse of "pederasty," did not make him pause. Consequently, the light which he has thrown upon the subject of this treatise only illuminates the dark dens of male vice in a big city. He leaves us where we were about the psychological and ethical problem. He shows what deep roots the passion strikes in the centers of modern civilization, and how it thrives under conditions at once painful to its victims and embarrassing to an agent of police.

Writers on forensic medicine take the next place in the row of literary witnesses. It is not their business to investigate the psychological condition of persons submitted to the action of the laws. They are concerned with the law itself, and with those physical circumstances which may bring the accused within its operation, or may dismiss him free from punishment.

The leading writers on forensic medicine at the present time in Europe explain more details on the subject in which I will not be able to talk much about it here for England. The author is so reticent upon the subject of unnatural crime that his handbook contain on "The Principles and Practice of Medical Jurisprudence" does not demand minute examination. It may, however, be remarked that he believes false accusations to be even commoner in this matter than in the case of rape, since they are only too frequently made the means of blackmailing. For this reason he leaves the investigation of such crimes to the lawyers.

Their last revision, would probably have been altered, had not the jurists felt that the popular belief in the criminality of pederasts ought to be considered. Consequently, a large number of irresponsible persons, in the opinion of experts, are still exposed to punishment by laws enacted under the influence of vulgar errors.

These writers are not concerned with the framing of codes, nor again with the psychological diagnosis of accused persons. It is their business to lay down rules whereby a medical authority, consulted in a doubtful case, may form his own view as to the guilt or innocence of the accused. Their attention is therefore mainly directed to the detection of signs upon the bodies of incriminated individuals.

To get the accurate justice, this question of physical diagnosis leads them into a severe critique. Their polemic attacks each of the points which he attempted to establish. I must content myself by referring to the passage of their work which deals with the important topic. Suffice it here to say that they reject all signs as worse than doubtful, except a certain deformation of one part of the body, which may possibly be taken as the proof of habitual prostitution, when it occurs in quite young persons. of course they admit that wounds, the guilt, violent abrasions of the skin, in certain places, and some syphilitic affections strongly favor the presumption of a criminal act. Finally, after insisting on the insecurity of alleged signs, and pointing out the responsibility assumed by physicians who base a judgment on them, the two experts sum up their conclusions in the following words

"It is extremely remarkable that while mention the cases, and communicates a select list of which appear to him to exhibit these peculiar conformations of the organs, he can only produce one single instance where the formation seemed indubitable. Let anyone peruse his cases, and he will be horrified at the unhesitating condemnations pronounced by. The two notes of exclamation which close this sentence in the original are fully justified. It is indeed horrifying to think that a person, implicated in some foul accusation, may have his doom fixed by a doctrinaire like Antipathy and ignorance in judges and the public, combined with erroneous canons of evidence in the expert, cannot fail to lead in such cases to some serious miscarriage of justice.

Passing from the problem of diagnosis and the polemic against it must be remarked that was the first writer of this class to lay down the distinction between inborn and acquired perversion of the sexual instinct. The law does not recognize this distinction. If a criminal act be proved, the psychological condition of the agent is legally indifferent—unless it can be shown that he was clearly mad and irresponsible, in which case he may be consigned to a lunatic asylum instead of a jail. But having studied the question of sexual maladies in general, and given due weight to the works of experts call attention to the broad differences which exist between persons in whom abnormal appetites are innate and those in whom they are acquired. Their companion sketches of the two types deserve to be translated and presented in a somewhat condensed form . . . In the majority of persons who are subject to this vice, it is congenital; or at any rate the sexual inclination can be followed back into the years of childhood, like a kind of physical. So, the paragraph tell us what sexual-violent and inversion can do to any serious human health.

The energy to heal is another way for any human being to get himself together. When I learned about human souls and the people who were specializing in restoring damaged energy in the spirit world, I was curious about how these souls might apply their unconscious spiritual knowledge when they were working in physical form. Some places create emphasis on this aspect of their skill development to help human beings at the right place also at the right time. My case is point and case is that those that do kind of work can also kidnap a human soul, while sleeping or anyway how. However, we only know a little idea of the source of their spiritual power to heal. The spiritual name could not be mentioned and during adjustment are necessary for incarnates as well as reincarnate.

Despite the conscious and unconscious in our life, the energy we receive have meaning because the energy we receive from the sun that make us grow and let us be alive. The accumulation of the energy may have different interpretation on each man or woman to see how each man was brave in his own accountability. No doubt about it, the humans have involved on the earth for long time and they always existed, the echo and the remaining of the each human before he or she depart from the earth is always remain on the spot of the life location, another human can pick up when he stop and continue. The energy to heal will automatically pick up when it rich the stage. So we can think of it that way that with all of our prayer and any other method we use to better our live will be additional to the echo.

As a transformers we do repair jobs on earth, we are the cleanup crew, transforming bodies to good Earth. There are people on earth who have gray spots of energy which cause them to get stuck. You see it when they make the same mistakes over and over in life. The experts will say my job is to incarnate, find them and try and remove these blocks so they make better decisions and gain confidence and self value. We transform them to be more productive people. Perhaps that is what they learn from their believers. When one race go down the popular has to go out to help the other so there is no mistakes; that is why the investment is good.

My health is great because of all the medication I have been taking for the past twenty years is quiet something, many things have pass away and many water have flow pass under the bridge. I travel a lot and been know that travel is better than to stay in one spot. During the weekend I could see that the town was quiet people stay home to do the house work while I am at work. The building will be so empty, some employee may show up for overtime work, but not many of them, maybe two or three employee will show up and before noon they all gone. On Sunday I will not expected any visitor, it will remain me and the building to watch. As a security guard officer, I must be vigilant for any intruder that might show up, sometimes I get scared in the building when it remain me alone. I will pick up phone and call my girl friend just to see someone to talk to. It is a bur-en job, but is good for student while I was in the school. I do my homework after I made my round inside the building and outside the building just to make sure everything is secure to the best of my ability.

Cycle dad do same thing every year without realizing is doing same thing over and over again. We work our self from studio apartment to a two bedroom apartment, from rat house to place where there is no rats, confusion over confusion, fight over fight in other to be descent among other people. We take on any job we can work with just give him time is the best answer to our prayer, give him six month he'll have what he wants. Out of that cafe the live could be normal. Every time you turn on the television is like its you they are talking about on television, is that a good thing or bad thing. To be sincere I don't know what they happy about if they can realized that it dehumanize. Some people behave as if they were in real life, had to believe, the world is round, for instance we see many cases about the animals life and life of the fish in the water, they are so proud of themselves when they are together, but when they see a human being or the predator, they get scared and ran away. When the animal get killed the body remain right there on the spot, but we did not know anything about their soul though to find out something like that we must first and try and save our own soul.

It was a big brown man that said he saw something in my dream, they never realize where you are coming from they can only try to know where you are going. Year after years, month after months, and day after days, I don't know what he saw in me that was so surprising. ·Suddenly my wife become a warehouse and don't want to listen to me anymore. Perhaps he thinks I was making money in America, I told him that if you can just listen to me for some minute, all the money in America will not run away but he get doing what is doing, disturbing while asleep in the night, dream after dream, noise after noise, When you are outside and I was inside and yet I was curious of some suspicious in fact I became nutritious and superstitious. The outside influences is much greater when nobody was there to protect you from the danger, and you don't know anything, even from inside, the insider enemy are also dangerous. The folk people know how to deal with their own problem.

As with Mr. right, I know that he could be thinking that if I didn't brought you out of the negro life you can not be a head, well, if you believe in God, you know that with God everything is possible. Anywhere you are you will definitely come across your own luck. Your predicament is never any mans dream. To be appreciated of some sought to a reason is to give thanks to God and other people that help you to succeed. You may have already have some grievances without realizing it or looking for way to get pass by it, In trying to help others or you know that what you are doing is not right but you insist on doing it anyway. In a strange land when the Marshall of the town say you do something improper that is what people will believe because that is what they are paying him for. However, you started to dance into a music that is not right and not concern you and what they are saying is that you will go to jail for a long time. Now you have a representative to represent you in a court of law, then how did the message get out to the other side of the country, by rumors or by representative to the chief of the country. The message transfer from one country to another. Moreover if everybody was talking about something that didn't concern you is only you know what they are saying, the world is for ever change. The whole country is not what it use to be. Every-body, people build more houses and more roads and children in the country, the life move faster. Now consider the scenario that country can fight each other without proper information, some people never think of causing trouble when you know you can not do this task by yourself. Now you come and be proud of what is impossible to achieved, if you could do it, then what happen or where were you then, those are the question you need to ask yourself. Where there is no man, God is there. You work during the day and you sleep at night, simple, but occasionally you would like to go to a party at night with the people that their culture permitted such occasions. You can be at the party as long as you like till morning or midnight or you can go to work for night shift which is all night. You can also work during the day and fixed your party during the day, that does not have something to do with the differences between day or night, obvious no, what you do in the day can also be done at night except loosing the night sleep, and may weakening the body. Remember when I came in with my coat and nice dress, I told you right there in the restaurant I never known nothing and I don't aim to know. I don't give a d urn how hard either try to make it, I kept my idea of doing things to myself, but now you all pushing me against the wall trying to constitute judges against my life, telling me how to run my life while in reality you will go and you will have to come in your own time and by then we would have already get what we wants. Why didn't you find it, because it wasn't there, how did you know wasn't there because some said so, so the time for wasting time is over. Contrary to the behaves that you have to dream every night in other to remember what you need to do in the day time, was ridiculous, to my opinion that dreams also affect the blood stream when you did not have enough sleep it could trigger the thinking of some thing else which can result in a lost of many thing in the body.

I am not an expert on medical line but I can tell you from experience that dream is not good especially those that seek the dream, it lead from one thing to another. So farseeing to dream and to know what tomorrow will bring is a real problem. The dream itself is a part of our soul, more importantly, the events that test us in life is our reaction to these events and how we handle the consequences. This is the primary reason for conscious amnesia. I have indicated that the soul is not usually shown all the alternatives to probable future events in the life to come. There good reasons for this practice despite spontaneous spiritual memory recall which is exist with some people. Amnesia allows for free will and self determination without the constraints of unconscious flashback memories about what we viewed in the in our world. I know past life regression who have had numerous experiences of heroic souls who volunteered to participate in the holocaust in any war camp. Some time thing could be prevented, but what will happen will happen. Perhaps this is because so many of these souls from the death camps are now living new lives in a new country. There are option for all kinds of disasters. For the bad ones, sometimes souls are prepared for what lies ahead for them by attending pr-life rehearsals, as illustrated by this statement.

There is a great need for ethicist souls, The society itself can not said is first come first serve, it can be said that there are reasons for the actions of some people turning out badly because of an underdeveloped soul, while the soul is still concentrate on preexisting conditions, solution as allies, friends, coworkers and they can said is co-existing with a disturbed human brain. Because of these conditions our free will toward making good choices could be more inhibited. Not until they were patronize to change for the better. I have tried to show that in the spirit world souls do not use this argument as a valid excuse for the lack of control over emotions in a host body.

The solution for all of us is to improve by staying with the process of continuing evolution to become better than we are, some people work toward their own advantage, I believe that is childish when we talk about the soul. If we know the reason why we are here and where we are going it will be a different case entirely. Our spirit guards were once just like us before they attained their current status. We are given many host bodies that we bring when we were born and gradually grow up, everything was perfect to us and for the others all of them are imperfect. Rather than being obsessive about a body which will only last one lifetime, concentrate on the evolution of your soul self and rely on your spiritual power. As we do this our capability for connecting with others will evolve and eventually cut through the dilemma of moral distinction that were articulated by the soul.

There are different types of soul as I said before, specialty the souls that represents a broad classification of souls with many sub groups. Harmony, nevertheless, while I try to pay attention to the minds of so many people, I do see an interdependence and connection behind all soul specialties. Souls in the general category of harmonizers often incarnate as communicators working in a variety of capacities. When they are discriminated beings, I am told they work as restorers of disrupted energy in their locations. Incarnating Harmonizer souls might be statesmen, prophets, inspirational messengers, negotiators, artists, musicians and writers. Typically, they are souls who balance the energy of planetary events involving human relationships. They may be public of private figures who operate behind the stage of world events. These souls are not healers in the traditional mode of working with individuals because Harmonizers function on a larger scale in attempting to diffuse negative energy.

In this case the health is very importance for someone who know the value. There many ways you can and different step you can take to heal yourself. You can go and see your doctor regularly, or go to your traditional healer for your safety, also the religious group maybe the best choice for you to take such as church, mosque and others, there are so may choices you can choose from. Now we will talk more about this topic spiritual healer later.

The indoor environment affects the comfort, health, and productivity of the people. People in a developed countries spend most of their time indoors, so most of the adverse exposure that they encounter regularly take place indoors. In environment for workers, many exposures that are potentially hazardous to health are exposures to substance emitted indoors from indoor sources. Dirt s, with air-conditions and heat, Such emissions can occur from building materials, from products used or stored indoors, from processes that occur in door environments from the micro organisms, insects, other animals and plants that live indoors and from the behavior of building occupants. Because of the contributions from indoor sources, indoor levels of many pollutants are higher than those attributable to indoor sources, buildings from outdoor air.

Another important point you needs to remember is about your health, climate is the condition of the environment for those that live in the area of cold and hot weather, it is necessary to be ready for each season when is approaching because during the cold winter the environment will be very cold and you will need a heater to support yourself. Without enough heat, you can get sick and if you don't take notice from there you can be getting sick from one disease to another, you will need to keep yourself wormed. Also when summer approaching, the floor pollution from the winter can also be hazardous to you health being. Take notice to the statement in the next paragraph and see what pollution can do to you.

Outdoor air temperature, humidity, air quality, precipitation and land surface wetness can all influences the indoor environment, depending on such factors as the integrity of a buildings are. The state of its heating's ventilation and air conditioning systems, the inhabitants of the outdoor ecosystem, and the characteristics of the buildings around it. If climate conditions in a particular area change for example, if the climate becomes warmer or if there are more server or more frequent episodes of high heat or intense precipitation build up, and other infrastructure that were designed to operate under the cold conditions may not function well under the strange weather

Furthermore, In responding to climate changes, The weather prediction may know what lies ahead but how will people co-operate, people and societies will seek to mitigate undesirable changes and adapt to changes that cannot be mitigated. Some of their responses will play out in how built spaces are designed, constructed, used, maintained, and in some cases retrofitted, and the actions taken may well have consequences for indoor environmental quality and the public health. Children spend a high proportion of their time in school, and they are consider more vulnerable than adults to the health effects of air pollution. The adult spend most of their time indoor in their residences, indoor environments occupied by the elderly or where health care is provided would be of special concern because those who are in fragile health are more vulnerable to further stresses than those who are healthy.

Some scientists are researching the history of the Earth's climate, many ancient records exist that give clues to the climate changes thousands of years ago. Scientist may used many form of tools to prove and search how the climate changes has been moving and affecting the human being and their health. Computer tool showed that the differences in temperatures could be due to two changes in the Earths orbit. These changes were the earth had a slightly greater shift on its axis and that the closest approach to the sun was made in a different time rather than how it was before. The effects of the changes in shift was that the northern continent received about 5 percent more heat from the sun in the summer and 5 percent less in the winter than it was today. The temperature differences between the ocean and the land were normal during that period. The changes in the wind caused more rainfall during the monsoon season. Just as plants and animals were beginning to be able to survive and repopulated due to the remaining of the ice age.

In northern latitudes the temperature plummeted once again with the cooling effects over the North Atlantic Ocean. The melting of these ice sheets produce and enormous influx of fresh water into the ocean, and since fresh water freezes more rapidly than salt water, a fast cover of winter ice may have formed on the ocean, diverting the normal flow of the gulf stream into the North Atlantic, the warmer water of the gulf stream that usually moderate cold winter temperature in North Western Europe were blocked causing changes in condition of the weather, and therefore affecting the health of the people.

As shown in the movies, and on TV, another perfect example of the climate change is when the dinosaurs dominated the world, temperatures were significantly warmer. The result of such studies have been difficult to interpret because the continents have drifted since that time and because different climate tools have been used, to get the accurate result. Since then it appears that Antarctica was free of ice, that the North poles was warm enough for strange fish to live there; and that tropical plants thrived at high rate. When climate change strange thing will started to appear, different thing such strange animals and strange fish will started to appear and reproduce.

The carbon dioxide in the air atmosphere has been increased over the last half of century. There are several reasons for this, deforestation in many parts of the world continues to progress at a rate far beyond growing trees even to replenished. This is important because trees prevent excess amounts of carbon dioxide from entering the atmosphere and give off oxygen as a byproducts of photosynthesis. In addition, the human population of the earth has been growing steadily larger with a current head count of approximately 5 billion. People need cleared land on which to live and to grow crops. Also more fossil fuels are being burned, especially in heavily industrialized countries, adding to the carbon dioxide content of the atmosphere.

The climate change show that a significant increases in carbon dioxide in the air would cause the upper levels of the earth's atmosphere to hold onto heat causing so called greenhouse effect. This would produce a warmer climate worldwide. The greenhouse warming occurs because sunlight can easily enter the earth's atmosphere and warm the ground and infrared radiation given off by the warmed surface of the earth cannot escape from the atmosphere. Some people think that without the greenhouse the earth will be too cold to live. At any rate, the climate changing also affecting the health of the people.

The major contributors to the greenhouse effect are the use of fossil fuels, gas smell, group of chemicals companies and other companies that produces a high level of carbon dioxide and other toxic gases. There is a natural capturing of heat due to the atmosphere water vapor surrounding the surface of the earth. All these contribute to warming climate. The human health depends on the climate that allow the people to enjoy the weather, possibly adapt to the situation; if minimize, but anything beyond control, there is nothing anyone can do about that. Your health is important and when we take care of our surrounding, we should be able to enjoy the weather.

As I was saying before, the norms and the folklore can be said that it comes from experience, physical, mentally and memory of the society. Everything is a moderation, the norms was recognize when two different society meet, the norm quickly feasible to both of them. We can interpret the soul in the different ways the ghost, the abandoned soul, the spirit soul, emotional soul, reuniting soul, and also wicked soul that must revenge. Should lead us to unthinkable mistake, or purposely do bad thing and to face the judgment is another soul entirely that must judge the case the way he see fit. Maybe, I said maybe, one day we might be able to returned the lost soul back to the rightful owner, and be perfectly match. The soul of been alive, the soul of living things.

In this modern lives, nonliving things can be restore such as trees, stone, and man made creature. The differences between the living things and nonliving things is the soul. When every thing stop, not working, it become nonliving things, but when its working as mechanical devices is a living-thing. Compare the space with my example, they say there is nothing in the space or a planet like ours Earth, can we harbor a new place in the Universe that has nothing as a living things!, If possible then there is a possibility to refined the idea.

I remember how my friend once said that the world's of you never really lose forever, the men who loved and lost them; probably because they and all of you don't want to. Not me nor a hundred of me, I said, the only thing to do is to get completely shut of them, abolish them. In my dream, I herd of tigers suddenly appears in the county, it will be better to have them shut up and watch them, even if you do lose the arms or leg ever time you get within ten feet of the wire, than to have them roaming and strolling loose all over ever where in the entire country. I wasn't born when uncle left for war so as far as I know his hair had already began to turn gray when I first saw him. Because although I was born by then, I couldn't remember him when he came home from war and to get ready to go back to it. So my friend both first and the second, when the opportunities lost it can never be regain that is old idea, though some people still stuck with it, nothing is in possible, just be aware of selfishness.

The health is an important part of the body, so we all wondered what he was using to live on, for money, sitting apparently all day long, day after day through the rest of the summer, winter on the flimsy porch of the little rented house. Looking at the river, also waiting for people to pass by, which he could not go back, or go forward and if he haven't have courage enough, he might have kill himself. No one would loan him that kind of money and the live is not heading anywhere.

When you are working then you can get people or the company to loan you money, otherwise, nobody will loan somebody not working. So when you see a stranger you don,t have to be wherry about them. You must be physically fit to do something important, otherwise thinking about hunger and also thinking how to solve a problem, it is a difficult situation to achieved something good. As a matter of fact, some people forget that the stranger sometimes bring business, the idea of another culture, and sometime they pay taxes, the folks may be suspicious of stranger because of the folklore, but never to be worry much, it all for the best. Perhaps stranger were driving out from his society to look for himself else where.

Sex is another important message for the people's health. There are different sex stereo type that we familiar with. Start from male and female, sexiest and sexuality, everything is moderation. *Gender* is the perceived component of human sexuality while *sex* is the biological or genetic component. Differentiating gender from sex allows social scientists to study influences on sexuality without confusing the social and psychological aspects with the biological and genetic aspects. As discussed below, gender is a social construction. If a social scientist were to continually talk about the social construction of sex, which biologists understand to be a genetic trait, this could lead to confusion.

Many species of living things are divided into two or more categories called **sexes**. These refer to complementary groups that combine genetic material in order to reproduce, a process called sexual reproduction. Typically, a species will have two sexes: *male* and *female*. The female sex is defined as the one to bear the offspring because she carry the pregnant for certain months, reproductive cell, and which bears the offspring. The categories of sex are, therefore, reflective of the reproductive functions that an individual is capable of performing at some point during its life cycle. And some other lay their eggs to hatch through the sun heat.

In mammals and many other species sex is determined by the sex chromosomes, called X and Y. For mammals, males typically have one of each (XY), while females typically have two X chromosomes (XX). All individuals have at least one X chromosome, the Y chromosome is generally shorter than the X chromosome with which it is paired, and is absent in some species. In humans, *sex* is conventionally perceived as a dichotomous state or identity for most biological purposes, such that a person can only be *female* or *male*.

Gender is the socially constructed component of human sexuality. *Gender* is an inner feeling that you are male, female, both, neither, or somewhere in between. Perhaps the best way to understand gender is to understand it as a process of social presentation. Because gender roles are delineated by behavioral expectations and norms, once individuals know those expectations and norms, the individual can adopt behaviors that project the gender he/she wishes to portray. One can think of gender like a role in a theatrical play—there are specific behaviors and norms associated with genders just like there are lines and movements associated with each character in a play. Adopting the behaviors and norms of a gender leads to the perception that someone belongs in that gender category. Gender roles are, unlike sex, mutable, meaning they can change. Gender is not, however, as simple as just choosing a role to play but is also influenced by parents, peers, culture, and society.

Parents sometimes socialize a biological boy (XY chromosomes) into what is perceived as a traditionally masculine role, that includes characteristics like:

independence, courage, and aggressiveness. Likewise, parents may socialize a biological female (XX chromosomes) into what is perceived as a traditionally feminine role, that includes characteristics like: submissiveness, emotionality, and empathy. Assuming both children feel like their gender roles fit their identities, the masculine boy and feminine girl will behave in ways that reflect their genders. For instance, the boy may play with toy soldiers and join athletic teams. The girl, on the other hand, may play with dolls and bond with other girls in smaller groups.

However, gender is fluid and can change. This can be seen by continuing the above example. It is possible for the boy to decide later in life that he no longer wishes to portray himself as traditionally masculine. The boy may adopt some traditionally feminine characteristics and become a feminist, or may adopt a feminine persona altogether Either change would involve adopting the behaviors and norms that go along with the intended gender. The same is true for the girl, who may adopt masculine characteristics.

A significant proportion of the human population does not correspond exclusively to either *female* or *male* genders or sexes. When gender identity and biological sex conflict, the result is sex *discordance*. Some discordance are purely biological, such as when the sex of the chromosomes (*genetic sex*) does not match the sex of the external genital. For more extensive discussion of this type of discordance, lack of coordinate between the biological sex and psychosocial gender components of gender, such as when the gender does not match the anatomic sex, are even more common but less well understood. The vast majority of people who are discordant in some aspect of psyche or behavior do not have any detectable biological inter-sex condition. Human societies respond to, or accommodate, these behavioral and psychological discordance in many different ways, ranging from suppression and denial of difference to acknowledging various forms of *third sex*

Some societies identify youths with atypical behavioral characteristics and, instead of giving them corrective therapy or punishing them, socialize them in such a way that their individual characteristics let them provide a useful function for the society in a recognized and respected role. Some of the roles these individuals may assume include.

Gender lack of coordinate leads to the understanding that what we traditionally understand to be feminine and masculine characteristics are social and cultural constructions. Some people have sought to define their sexuality and sexual identity in the belief that the simple division of all humans into *males* and *females* does not fit their individual conditions. We recognize two sexes: male, female, from there we can distinguish sexuality, bisexual, homosexual, and more Although quickly rejected as a bizarre flouting of human nature and social reality and inimical to the interests of those whom she was attempting to champion, it expresses the difficulty and imperfection of the current social responses to these variations.

While much of this chapter focuses on the socially constructed differences between men and women, it is also important to note there are some clear physiologically differences between the two sexes. In addition to different sex organs and sex chromosomes, the average male is 10 percent taller, 20 percent heavier, and 35 percent stronger in the upper body than the average female. Some researchers believe that these physiological differences may have been influenced by social/cultural decisions in our evolutionary past. Even so, when measured against their own body size, rather than on an absolute scale how much women can carry relative to their body size versus how much men can carry relative to their body size, actual strength differences are minimal.

Women, for reasons still somewhat undetermined, tend to outlive men. Some believe this difference is due to the riskier lifestyles of men, especially earlier in life, combined with their typically more physically stressing occupations. Behaviorally, age of sitting, teething, and walking all occur at about the same time in men and women. There are no significant differences in intelligence, happiness, or self-esteem between men and women. However, women are, statistically, twice as vulnerable to anxiety disorders and depression, but only one-third as vulnerable to suicide and one-fifth as vulnerable to alcoholism.

Much evidence has shown that there are differences in male and female brains. In fact, the temporal lobe, which is the part of the brain associated with language and emotion, develops up to 4 years earlier in girls in comparison to boys. On the other hand, the left parietal lobe, which is associated with mathematical and spatial reasoning, is thought to develop up to 4 years earlier in boys. This difference could account for the fact that girls are sometimes thought to be better when it comes to language and are more emotional, while boys are thought to be better in math. As well, some say that girls are better at hearing than boys. A typical teenaged girl hears up to 7 times better than a typical teenaged boy. This could possibly explain why boys are diagnosed with ADHD more often. Lastly there is a difference between sight for girls and boys. Girls are able to see facial expressions / emotions better while boys are able to see motion better. Girls use the p-cells in the retina, which are associated with texture and color, while boys use m-cells, which are associated with motion.

As the previous section outlined, some gender differences are attributable to biology. However, there are a number of gender differences that vary by society, environment, and/or culture, indicating they are social heritage. For example, in work group situations in the U.S., men tend to focus on the task at hand whereas women tend to focus more on personal relationships. When eating, women eating with men tend to eat fewer calories than when they are eating with women. Both of these differences in behavior vary by culture and are therefore believed to be socially constructed. Two detailed examples of socially constructed gender differences are presented below: workforce differences and education.

An often discussed and debated difference between men and women involves work and occupations. Woman's participation in the workforce has varied significantly over time. Prior to the development of capitalism and factory-type work, women played a significant role in food production and household maintenance. With the advent of capitalism and labor outside of the home, women continued to play a significant role, though their participation in paid labor outside the home initially diminished. Also, w omen's participation in the labor force varied, depending on marital status and social class.

Current U.S. labor force statistics illustrate woman's changing role in the labor force. For instance, since 1971, women participation in the labor force has grown tremendously over the decades. Women also make, on average, $17,000 less than do men. Women tend to be concentrated in less prestigious and lower paying occupations that are traditionally considered woman's *jobs* Finally, women are not paid the same wages as men for similar work ... Women tend to make between 75% and 91% of what men make for comparable work, though it depends on how the comparison is made. For instance, college educated women between 26 and 45 earned 74.7 cents in hourly pay for every dollar men in the same group made in 2005. However, if you compare women and men with similar profiles and qualifications, the gap is smaller: women make about 91% of what men make, at least they have since the 1980s. In the 1970s, similarly qualified women made only 82% as much as their male counterparts.

However, at all educational and skill levels, women still make less than men, The women earn less than men with equal qualifications helps explain why women are enrolling in college at higher rates than are men—they require a college education to make the same amount as men with a high school diploma. Men tends to use their skill than women do

The gap between men and women wages narrowed during the 1980s and mid 1990s, but that momentum has fallen off and the distance now appears to have stagnated. The gap in income between genders used to be similar between middle-class and affluent workers, but it is now widest among the most highly paid. A woman making in the 95th percentile in 2006 would earn about $95,000 per year; a man in the 95th earning percentile would make about $115,000, a 28% difference (and that's not including the highest earners, who are predominantly men. The narrowing of the gap in pay has also been called into question. While it appears there has been a narrowing of the gap in pay between men and women, Mulligan and Rubinstein show that much of the narrowing is actually the result of the most able women entering the workforce and not decreases in the pay gap between men and women. Thus, even the apparent narrowing of pay between the sexes likely overestimates the actual differences in pay.

It is quite difficult for women to climb to the top in the business world. For instance, only 3% of tech firms and just 1% of high-tech firms were founded by women and very few are headed by women. But the women who do climb to the top of the organizational ladder in business also experience both overt and covert discrimination. For instance, companies with women on the board of directors have lower stock evaluations than do companies with exclusively male boards. This is likely a reflection of the lack of shareholder trust in women. Women are also often put into leadership positions in corporations when companies are in a crisis and have little hope for recovery, resulting in poorer evaluations of women in leadership positions. The phenomenon of putting women into leadership positions when companies are in trouble is referred to as "the glass cliff" and is also observed in politics, as women are disproportionately chosen to run in elections when it is almost guaranteed that the incumbent male candidate will win.

The most common explanation for the wage gap between men and women is the finding that women pay a motherhood wage penalty, regardless of whether or not they are actually mothers. You can think about this from the perspective of a potential employer: If you have two equally qualified candidates for a position, both are in their mid-twenties, married, and straight out of college, but one is a male and the other is female, which would you choose? Many employers choose men over women because women are "at risk" of having a child, even though they may not want to have children. And, of course, to the potential employer accommodating a pregnant woman and mother is more cumbersome than a male turned father (despite the obvious need for children to continue our species). Thus, women pay a penalty for their ability to give birth. Additionally, when women do have children, this often requires a period of time outside the workforce, whether it's six weeks or several months. Employers take the time off into account when considering raises. The "Mommy track" often results in women making less money than equally qualified men who have been in the same job for the same amount of time because women take time off to have children and are often responsible for taking care of children while men rarely do so. Thus, women are often paid less despite having the same qualifications because they are) at risk of having children or do have children and are penalized for doing so.

Another possible explanation for the wage gap between men and women has recently been proposed—customer bias towards white males. Found that customers who viewed videos featuring a black male, a white female, or a white male actor playing the role of an employee helping a customer were 19% more satisfied with the white male employee's performance and also were more satisfied with the store's cleanliness and appearance, despite the fact that all three actors performed identical, read the same script, and were in the exact same location with identical camera angles and lighting. They provide further evidence to support this claim by noting that white male doctors are rated as more approachable and competent than other doctors. They interpret their findings to suggest that employers are willing to pay more for white male employees because employers are customer driven and customers are happier with white male employees. They also suggest that what is required to solve the problem of wage inequality isn't necessarily paying women more but changing customer biases.

Additional reasons for disparity in pay are discussed below.

Another factor that may contribute to the higher wages of white men is the number of job leads they receive. White men, particularly those in management positions, receive more job leads from friends and colleagues than do white women and Hispanic men and women. Black men and women receive about as many job leads and tips, but only for non-management jobs. As many jobs result from social networking, white males are advantaged by their higher number of job leads, potentially contributing to their higher salaries and more prestigious jobs.

Another often studied difference between men and women is educational attainment. For a long time, higher education undergraduate and graduate education was an exclusively male bastion. Women did eventually gain access to institutions of higher learning, but parity or equality on a number of levels has still not been achieved. One measure of educational attainment where women have made great inroads is in college attendance. In 1960, 37.9% of female high school graduates enrolled in college, compared with 54.0% of male high school graduates. In 2002, more female high school graduates were enrolling in college than males, 68.4% of females vs. 62.1% males. in fact, made significant progress in this respect. Women now earn more Bachelors and Masters degrees than men do, and for the first time in 2009, they earned more PhD s. Women have made significant roads into some of this traditionally most prestigious professions as well: 40%

of medical school graduates are women and women make up large percentages of law school and students as well.

Despite the progress, there are still problems. While women are entering college at higher rates and even earning more degrees, the degrees are in less prestigious areas social sciences and humanities compared to physical sciences) and women with degrees still earn less than do men with comparable degrees. For instance, in medicine, women tend to concentrate in lower paying specialties dermatology and family medicine). The highest paid specialties are dominated by men and will be for decades to come, based on the pipeline of residents: 28% of radiology residents in 2004-5 were women, and only 10% of orthopedic surgery residents were.

At the primary and secondary levels, girls don't often do as well as boys, particularly in math and the sciences. One recent study offers a partial explanation for why this might be the case: highly math-anxious female teachers in elementary school pass their math-anxiety on to the girls in the classroom, but not to the boys. At the beginning of the class, there were no differences in math anxiety between the boys and girls, but in classes taught by female math-anxious teachers, girls developed math anxiety and boys did not. This anxiety led girls to believe boys were better at math than girls, though there is no evidence to suggest that is actually the case. sexism is discrimination against people based on their sex or gender. Sexism can refer to three subtly different beliefs or attitudes. The belief that one sex is superior to the other. The belief that men and women are very different and that this should be strongly reflected in society, language, the right to have sex, and the law. It can also refer to simple hatred of men or women.

Many peoples' beliefs on this topic range along a continuum. Some people believe that women should have equal access to all jobs. Others believe that while women are superior to men in a few aspects, in most aspects men are superior to women.

Sexist beliefs are an example of essentialist thought, which holds that individuals can be understood and often judged based on the characteristics of the group to which they belong; in this case, their sex group male or female. Essential ism assumes that all individuals clearly fit into the category of *male* or *female*, which is not the case. It also assumes characteristics are immutable, which is also not the case.

A good example of sexism against women is a question that has been asked in numerous surveys over the years in the US, "Would you vote for a female candidate for president?" A 2005 Gallup poll found that 92% of Americans would vote for a female candidate, but follow-up research found that this percentage was the result of response bias. When you use research techniques that allow people to express how they really feel toward women, the actual percentage who would not vote for a female candidate because she is female is closer to 26%. Intriguingly, it is not just men who feel that way, but some women, too. In short, nearly 1/4 of Americans maintain sexist attitudes against women.

Sexism against women is often called chauvinism though chauvinism is actually a wider term for any extreme and unreasonable partisanship toward a group to which one belongs, especially when the partisanship includes malice and hatred towards a rival group. Many forms of radical feminism can legitimately be referred to as *chauvinism*. This is not common usage, however, and the term is most often used to refer to male chauvinism.

While the view that women are superior to men is also sexism, only in recent years has an awareness of this reverse sexism begun to develop in public discourse. Certain forms of sexual discrimination are illegal in many countries, but nearly all countries have laws that give special rights, privileges, or responsibilities to one sex.

Recent research illustrates the pervasiveness of sexism in the media. found that sports coverage on major television networks focuses predominantly on men, despite the increase in female participation in sports since the passage of 1972. In 1971, 294,000 high school girls played interscholastic sports, compared to 3.7 million boys. By 1989 that ratio changed substantially—1.8 million girls played sports compared to 3.4 million boys. By 2004 the ratio had changed even more—2.9 million girls compared to 4.0 million boys. At the collegiate level, the change was also substantial. In 1972, the average college in the U.S. had two women sports teams. In just the four years between 2000 and 2004, universities in the U.S. added 631 new women teams.

Despite the increase in participation in sports, major network news coverage of woman's sports has changed very little over the last 15 years. In 1989 women garnered only 5% of air time; in 1999 that increased to 9%, but it fell back to 6% by 2005. Sports highlights shows ESPN S's Sport center are even less accommodating, giving only 2% to 3% of air time to women. What's more, the little amount of air time given to women often portrays woman's sports as "novelties" or pseudo-sports and often includes gags, like the women nude bungee jump in 1999. Additionally, much of the coverage of women in sports is sexless, as attention is often only given to women deemed "attractive" by the news anchors. Whether this treatment of women in sport is intentional or not, it is a clear example of sexism in the media.

The author attributed the differences in wealth distribution to historical instances of gender discrimination. Up until the 19th Century most women could not own property and woman's participation in the paid labor force outside the home was limited. It is possible that wealth among the elite may be redistributed toward a more equal balance between the sexes with increasing numbers of women entering the workforce and moving toward more financially lucrative positions in major corporations.

The differences in income between men and women mentioned above are partially due to discrimination, but also due, in part, to some women (including highly educated women) choosing to leave the labor force and stay home with their young children. Leaving the labor force doubly impacts income. It takes away immediate income, and reduces experience and tenure, lowering future earning potential. Additionally, while women have made significant inroads into many highly paid fields the influx of women into those fields has slowed since 2000.

Women in some organizations are suing their employers claiming gender discrimination. For instance, Walt Mart currently facing a lawsuit by some of its female employees who allege gender discrimination. Part of the plaintiffs' argument rests on the fact that, while roughly 75% of intra-store department heads are women, only 20% of store managers (who make close to $100,000 per year) are women. It is difficult to prove discrimination in such cases. In fact, many researchers point out that there may and probably are other root causes, including: differences in gender socialization (men believe they need to support their families as the primary breadwinners, leading to greater job commitment) and emphasis by the government on equality in pay and opportunity between genders.

Sexism can take many forms, including preventing women from attending college and paying women less than men for comparable work. Another common form of sexism is violence, especially violence toward women. In 2002, women were the victims of over 900,000 violent crimes and over 200,000 rapes or sexual assaults. Men are more likely to be the victims of violent crime, but far less likely to be the victims of rapes or sexual assaults.

Sociologists and other social scientists generally attribute many of the behavioral differences between genders to socialization. socialization is the process of transferring norms, values, beliefs, and behaviors to future group members. In gender socialization, the groups people join are the gender categories, *males* and *females*. Thus, gender socialization is the process of educating and instructing potential males and females as to the norms, behaviors, values, and beliefs of group membership.

Preparations for gender socialization begin even before the birth of the child. One of the first questions people ask of expectant parents is the *sex* of the child. This is the beginning of a social categorization process that continues throughout life. Preparations for the birth often take the infant's sex into consideration. Many of the gender differences just described are attributed to differences in socialization, though it is possible genetic and biological factors play some role. It is important to keep in mind that gender differences are a combination of social and biological forces; sometimes one or the other has a larger influence, but both play a role in dictating behavior.

One illustration of early life gender socialization can be seen in preschool classrooms. Children in preschool classrooms where teachers were told to emphasize gender differences saw an increase in stereotyped views of what activities are appropriate for boys and girls, while children with teachers who did not emphasize gender showed no increase. This study supports the idea that subtle cues that surround us in our everyday lives strongly influence gender socialization.

Research finds that gender differences in work and occupations begin with adolescents' first jobs:

- first jobs are significantly segregated by sex
- girls work fewer hours per week than boys
- girls earn less per hour than boys
- hourly wages are higher in job types dominated by males
- girls are assigned more housework than are boys

Researchers attribute these differences to gender socialization and differential opportunities for boys and girls.

Another example of research finding differences in behavior between genders can be seen in the differences in self-ratings of attractiveness. Using fifty-five Johns Hopkins University undergraduates the authors had the students fill out questionnaires they designed as self-appraisals of attractiveness. The authors then used a panel to rate the attractiveness of the participants (an objective measure). The researchers found that women are fairly accurate in their assessments of their attractiveness but men are not. They explained their findings by discussing the salience of attractiveness for women, a characteristic learned through socialization: Attractiveness is a more important component of woman's lives then man's. This is seen in the disparity between men and women in the number of cosmetic surgeries they undergo. Of the 11.5 million cosmetic surgeries performed in 2005, women accounted for 85% to 90% of them. Because attractiveness is so important for women, they are more attuned to their actual attractiveness than are men.

Social biologist and evolutionary psychologist argue that much of social life as we know it today has roots in human evolution and biology. According to these theories, some of the gender differences in behavior are attributable to differences in physiology. For instance, differences in sexuality and sex drives may be due to human evolution. Women, who physically invest more in the creation and bearing of children (through pregnancy), may have a greater propensity toward monogamous relationships as having a partner to help them improves the chances of their child's survival. Men, on the other hand, may be inclined less toward monogamy and more toward polygamous relationships as their investment in offspring can be far smaller than that of women. Evolutionary psychologists and sociobiology use this theory to explain differences in sexual behavior, attitudes, and attractions between men and women: women tend to be attracted to men who can provide support protection and resources and prefer fewer sexual partners than do men; men, on the other hand, are attracted to fertile women the symbols of which have changed over time and prefer more sexual partners.

In this perspective, which was developed in the 1940s and 1950s, genders are viewed as complementary—women take care of the home while men provide for the family. Much current research, especially after the woman's movement of the 1960s and 1970s, criticizes this approach for supporting the status quo and condoning the oppression of women

In contrast to the status quo supporting structural functionalist approach, social conflict theory argues that gender is best understood in terms of power relationships. Man's dominance of women is seen as an attempt to maintain power and privilege to the detriment of women. This approach is normative in that it prescribes changes to the power structure, advocating a balance of power between genders. (See also feminist theory

Different types of music have been known to make impacts on sexual behavior to different people and different ages. Types of music can calm people's senses down or fire them up; it can also be something that arouses people.

Studies have shown that there is a strong link between the music that young teens listen to and sexual behaviors. The average teen listens to 1.5 to 2.5 hours of music every day. Many of these songs have sexual themes that can range from being romantic and playful to raunchy and degrading.

Songs that depict men as sex studs and woman as sexual objects and have explicit references to sex acts are more likely to begin early sexual behavior than those where sexual references are more hidden and relationships appear more committed.

Teens who listened to lots of music with degrading sexual messages were almost twice as likely to start having intercourse or other sexual activities within the following two years as were teens who listened to little or no sexually degrading music. Girls who watch more than 14 hours of music videos are more likely to engage in unsafe sex with multiple partners and get STI. Boys who watch violent sex scenes on television have less sympathy to victims of sexual violence.

Among heavy listeners, 51 percent started having sex within two years, versus 29 percent of those who said they listened to little or no sexually degrading music.

A new research study discovered teenagers who preferred popular songs with degrading sexual references were more likely to engage in intercourse or in precoital activities.

The relationship between exposure to lyrics describing degrading sex and sexual experience held equally for both young men and women.

A study of more than 700 ninth-graders who listened to lyrics considered sexually degrading—and—linked the music to higher levels of sexual behavior among young teens."

The findings indicate that "people who are exposed to certain messages in music are more likely to copy or emulate what they hear,

University's research found that the brain's responses to music are just like it's responses to sex; the measured brain activity of someone who receives trembles from music and the measured brain activity of someone having pleasurable sex are exactly the same.

—Fans of different musical genres gave very different responses, with fans of hip-hop and dance music standing out in particular. 37.5% of hip-hop fans and 28.7% of dance music fans have had more than one sexual partner in the past five years,

The purpose of this discussion was to determine the effects of cognitive distortions concerning women on sexually aggressive behavior in the laboratory. Twenty-seven men listened to misogynous rap music and 27 men listened to neutral rap music. Participants then viewed neutral, sexual-violent, and assault film vignettes and chose one of the vignettes to show to a female confederate. Among the participants in the misogynous music condition, 30% showed the assaulter vignette and 70% showed the neutral vignette. In the neutral condition, 7% showed the sexual-violent or assault vignette and 93% showed the neutral vignette. Participants who showed the sexual-violent or assaulter stimuli reported that the confederate was more upset and uncomfortable in viewing these stimuli than did participants who showed the neutral vignette. These findings suggest that misogynous music facilitates sexually aggressive behavior and support the relationship between cognitive distortions and sexual aggression.

Studies from 10 years ago show that 60% of videos on MTV at the time contained sexual imagery and sexually suggestive content. A cross-sectional review of 40 randomly selected videos showed that 90% of the videos were sexually suggestive. Research results show that the more people watch music videos, the increased likelihood they are to have high frequency estimates of sexual behaviors and liberal attitudes toward sex. This is also coupled with a stronger tendency to endorse sex-role stereotypes and the toleration of sexual harassment.

Men watching rock or rap music video clips including texts using rough violence and direct sexual messages presented increased levels of testosterone, aggressiveness and misogynistic reactions. This then can lead to more violent or abusive sexual behaviors with their partners.

Those who enjoy jazz have 34% more sex than those who like pop and the least sexually active are those listening to classical music.

The rock and roll lifestyle has always been associated with sex and drugs. Musicians had always attracted attention from the opposite sex. While some rock groups were in favor of long-term relationships, other groups and artists did little to discourage it, and many tales of sexual acts became part of the rock music legacy.

Parental permissiveness, peer pressure, self-esteem, and poor at home environments are the most influential ways in which young adults acquire explicit sexual music. The role of a parenting and a positive at home environment can make a huge difference in the music of which an individual is listening to at a certain age. Music which is sold in stores can be marked explicit and cannot be bought by individuals under the age of 17. Enforcing that right can reduce music's influence of sexual behavior. Outside of the home, educators in the school systems must also make a positive environment in which explicit lyrics and music is not allowed. "A healthy home atmosphere is one that allows a child to investigate what pop culture has to offer and at the same time say 'I know this is a fun song but you know that it's not right to treat women this way or this isn't a good person to have as a role model.

Some specialist said "Kids who don't have a solid family and community value system to anchor them—they're the ones who are influenced by TV. They are living with a parent who is overwhelmed, they are disconnected from a cultural, religious or ethnic set of beliefs . . . so they learn how the world works from TV."

They monitor the music and watching of music videos

- They discuss sexual activity and the risks
- They discuss content of lyrics and possibility of actual happening (rape, using drugs or alcohol, etc
- Studies have shown that teens spend more time listening to music than watching television. Although music is viewed as a source of entertainment, it is important to recognize that listening habits influence coping

strategies, identity formation and interpersonal relationships.

When people hear songs depicting women this way and men that way, they begin to develop stereotypes about different genders. Through musical lyrics and music videos, gender and sexual stereotypes are formed and applied in society. In rap songs and videos women get depicted as objects that always have a sexual desire towards men and will be their servants, while men get depicted as strong, powerful, and rich. A major study out of Harvard University has found that popular music videos overwhelmingly portray black men as aggressors and white women as victims. The study analyzed 518 videos on the four most popular music video networks in the U.S. Researchers found that violence occurred in 14.7 per cent of the videos shown, with MTV showing the highest rate of violent videos at 22.4 per cent. In particular, black people were portrayed as aggressors in 25 per cent of the violent videos—95 per cent of them men. Of victims in the violent videos, 47 per cent were white women. Almost all of the aggressors (85 per cent) in the violent videos were portrayed as attractive role models, not villains.

For the conclusion and the quest of my story. What will profit a man if he rich and lost his soul, there is no right or wrong in the way man choose to spend his life, he will arrived to a conclusion; if it is a bad situation or good life; all depends how we spent our days. If a child appears to be having difficulty recovering any type of experience, parents may help prevent fears from growing by providing rewarding, happy and safe experience in any situation. Place of birth is very important, because that is where you originate from, your parents are their for you to help. Security guard get paid and protect the client facility. Security firm is a small business and a sustainability makes sense for the environment and for the business.

For small and big business, they all use computer for their day to day business, both in the warehouses and at home. Computer is a must have technology in this days of our modern life.

Cheating refers to immoral way of achieving a goal. It is generally used for the breaking of rule to gain advantage in a competitive situation and among ourselves.

Consider your health as important issue, among other things, many things associated with us that contribute a lot to our health. The weather, cool, sun, pollen(flower) and indoor pollution, all these type of weather can make our temperature go up and down. So we must careful for what can make us sick.

Another study investigated the sex-role stereotyping of occupational roles and the behaviors of music-video characters in a random sample of 182 MTV music videos. It was found that both male and female characters were shown in sex-typed occupations. Male characters were more adventuresome, domineering, aggressive, violent, and victimized than female characters, while females were more affectionate, dependent, nurturing, and fearful than males. It was also found that a large percentage of female characters wore revealing clothing and that they initiated and received sexual advances more often than males. An Investigation of Sex-Role Stereotyping in Music-Videos shows that throughout history, music has created influence in individuals all over the world. Athletes use music to excite them for competition, sleep deprived people use music to calm them down and fall asleep, and some people are influenced by music which arouses them sexually. Weaved inside of music's lyrics, beats, and rhythms, lies a deep sexual influence which affects many people. The beats and sounds of music can affect our motion while the lyrics attack our minds and place pictures and stereotypes in them. Music is a powerful sound which can create an incredible sexual mood, with an incredible sexual influence for better or for worse.

This book remind us what life is fee like, the author try to reveal some situations that you may go through in life and how to avoid some of the bad ones if you read this book. The first destiny exp lane so much real life situation, and this latest edition give you more broader view. It is not necessarily to take my word for it but if you read it, you might gain something.